Camouflaged Fist

Camouflage Smocks used by the Infantry Brigades of the 6th Armoured Division in Italy 1944

Gareth Scanlon

Helion & Company

Helion & Company Limited
Unit 8 Amherst Business Centre
Budbrooke Road
Warwick
CV34 5WE
England
Tel. 01926 499 619
Email: info@helion.co.uk
Website: www.helion.co.uk
Twitter: @helionbooks
Visit our blog http://blog.helion.co.uk/

Published by Helion & Company 2024
Designed and typeset by Mach 3 Solutions (www.mach3solutions.co.uk)
Cover designed by Paul Hewitt, Battlefield Design (www.battlefield-design.co.uk)

Text © Gareth Scanlon 2024
Photographs and illustrations © as individually credited. Any uncredited images © Gareth Scanlon

Every reasonable effort has been made to trace copyright holders and to obtain their permission for the use of copyright material. The author and publisher apologize for any errors or omissions in this work and would be grateful if notified of any corrections that should be incorporated in future reprints or editions of this book.

ISBN 978-1-804515-84-6

British Library Cataloguing-in-Publication Data.
A catalogue record for this book is available from the British Library.

All rights reserved. No part of this publication may be reproduced, stored in a retrieval system, or transmitted, in any form, or by any means, electronic, mechanical, photocopying, recording or otherwise, without the express written consent of Helion & Company Limited.

For details of other military history titles published by Helion & Company Limited contact the above address or visit our website: http://www.helion.co.uk.

We always welcome receiving book proposals from prospective authors.

The 'D-Day Dodgers' 1944

Sung to 'Refrain' of Lili Marlene

We're the D-Day Dodgers, out in Italy,
Always drinking vino, always on the spree,
Eighth army skivers, and the Yanks,
We live in Rome, we laugh at tanks,
For we're the D-Day Dodgers, in Sunny Italy.

We landed at Salerno, a holiday with pay,
Jerry brought his band down, to cheer us on our way,
They showed us the sights, and gave us tea,
We all sang songs, the beer was free,
To welcome us D-Day Dodging, in Sunny Italy.

Naples and Cassino, taken in our stride,
We didn't go to fight, we just went for the ride,
Anzio and the Sangro, are just names,
We only went to look for dames,
We're still D-Day Dodgers in Sunny Italy.

Once we had the Griff, that we were going home,
Back to dear old Blighty, never more to roam,
Then someone whispered, in France you'll fight,
We said "Blow that. We'll just sit tight",
The Windy D-Day Dodgers in Sunny Italy.

Looking 'round the mountains, in the mud and rain,
There's lots of little crosses, some which bear no name,
Blood, sweat and tears and toil are gone,
The boys beneath them slumber on ,
These are your D-Day Dodgers, who'll stay in Italy.[1]

William I. McKenzie, 'S' Company Scots Guards,
1st Guards Brigade, 6th Armoured Division.

**Dedicated to My Dadcu's
Who Both Served in 3rd Battalion, Welsh Guards**

Glyn Spowart

09.02.1916–07.02.2003

Samuel Davies

31.05.1914–28.02.1972

"*Cymru Am Byth*"

Contents

Abbreviations		vi
Foreword		ix
Preface		xi
Acknowledgements		xvi
Introduction		xviii
1	Italy: Geography & Climate and Impact on the Campaign	21
2	6th Armoured Division: Infantry Brigade Composition	33
3	Uniform and the Advent of the Camouflage Smocks	47
4	M1929 *Telo Mimetico* Camouflage	56
5	Evidence, Photographs and Chronology	61
6	Manufacture – 'C' Clothing & Repair Factory, Royal Army Ordnance Corps	96
7	Construction & Surviving Examples	110
8	Modern Images	124

Appendices

I	Photographs – The Changing Environment	167
II	Photographs – Uniform Worn by Infantrymen	173
III	Unconfirmed 6th Armoured Division Photographs	178
IV	M1929 *Telo Tenda* Booklet	180

Endnotes	182
Bibliography	187
About The Author	189

Abbreviations

2L&BH – 2nd Battalion Lothians & Border Horse
16/5L – 16th/5th Lancers
Adj – Adjutant
Adv – Advance
AFHQ – Allied Forces Headquarters
AM – Air Ministry
Arm – Armoured
Armd – Armoured
AT – Anti-Tank
A.Tk – Anti-Tank
Att – Attached
Battln – Battalion
BD – Battledress
Bde(s) – Brigade(s)
Bn – Battalion
Br – British
Br – Bridge
Brig – Brigadier
Capt – Captain
Cardiff Arms – Name awarded to 3rd Battalion Welsh Guards Leave Camp: Villa Pischiello near Passignano sul Trasimeno
CDN – Canada / Canadian
CG – Coldstream Guards
CIGS – Chief of the Imperial General Staff
Civ – Civilian
CMF – Central Mediterranean Forces
CM – Centimetre
Comd – Command
Coldm – Coldstream Guards
Coy(s) – Company(s)
DDOS – Deputy Director Ordnance Services
DOS – Director Ordnance Services
Div(s) – Division(s)
DSD – Director of Staff Duties
Ech – Echelon

ABBREVIATIONS

Est – Established
Fwd – Forward
Gall – Gallon / Gallons
Gds – Guards
Gdsm – Guardsman / Guardsmen
GG – Grenadier Guards
GHQ – General Headquarters
Gren – Grenadier (as in Grenadier Guards)
GS – General Service
GSGS – Geographical Section General Staff
Hosp – Hospital
Hrs – hours
IO – Intelligence Officer
KD – Khaki Drill
KG103 – Khaki Green Blanco Webbing Colouring
KG3 – Khaki Green Dark Blanco Webbing Colouring
IRTD – Infantry Reinforcement & Training Depot
LOB – Left Out of Battle
MECo – Mills Equipment Company
MG – Machine Gun
Movt – Movement
MSRU – Mobile Stores Repair Units
No.4 – Short Magazine Lee Enfield No.1 MkIV
Offrs – Officers
Offs – Officers
O Gp – Orders Group
OR – Other Ranks
Ord – Ordnance
Paras – Paragraphs
PAK – *Panzerabwehrkanone* German Anti-Tank Gun
Pl – Platoon
Pt – Point (number denotes height in metres)
PW – Prisoner of War
Pz – *Panzer*
PzGR– *Panzergrenadier*
QM – Quartermaster
RAF – Royal Air Force
RAOC – Royal Army Ordnance Corps
RB / R.B. – Rifle Brigade
Rds – Ammunition Rounds
REME – Royal Electrical and Mechanical Engineers
Rfts – Reinforcements
RSI – *Repubblica Sociale Italiana* (Pro-German Italian National Republican Army)
S Coy – Scots Guards Rifle Company attached to 2nd Battalion Coldstream Guards
SD – Service Dress
SG – Scots Guards

Sigs – Signals
SMLE – Short Magazine Lee Enfield Rifle No.1 MkIII
SP – Self Propelled (Gun)
Sp Coy – Support Company
Tac – Tactical
Thompson – Thompson Sub Machine Gun
Tks – Tanks
TMSG – Thompson Sub Machine Gun
TNA – The National Archives
Tps – Troops
Trg – Training
U/C – Under Command
WG – Welsh Guards
Wksps– Workshops

Foreword

For the British and Commonwealth Forces, the major land campaigns of the Second World War were fought in North Africa, North-West Europe, Italy and Burma. Much has been written of the first two campaigns and in recent years the latter campaign has rightfully gained significant and burgeoning attention. The Italian campaign has in contrast received the least coverage. With few rapid advances, colourful generals or stirring outflanking moves, the accounts are more often critical of strategic and tactical features of the campaign.

The campaign saw some of the hardest and most ferocious fighting of the war; in many instances more reminiscent of 1914–18 than of 1939–45. Discussion is usually prefaced by noting the harsh winter conditions, mountainous terrain dissected by numerous rivers, the presence of a large and vulnerable civilian population, destruction of cultural and artistic treasures, the consequent ease of defence by the German adversaries and the effect that all this had on the speed and success of operations. At the command level, there were the inevitable difficulties and controversies created by coalition warfare, and then an easy path to deride the flawed strategy, in light of the above limitations.

The campaign was fought by a multi-national force of British, Americans, Canadians, New Zealanders, Indians, Gurkhas, Poles, Rhodesians, South Africans, the French – including Algerians, Moroccans, Tunisians and Equatorial Africans – a Jewish Brigade from Palestine, and later Brazilians. Many of the troops had already seen combat in North Africa and were asked repeatedly to draw from the well of courage and go into battle for another hill, village or river crossing.

The Italian campaign still has significant resonance for those whose relatives fought in the campaign. My late father, Sydney Warwick, fought with 5th Battalion, Grenadiers Guards, of 24th Guards Brigade, in 1st British Infantry Division, at Anzio in January 1944, and then in the advance from south of Rome to the Apennines until February 1945 in 6th South African Armoured Division. Other relatives served in 6th Armoured Division, the focus of this book. An uncle served in 3rd Battalion, Grenadier Guards, in 1st Guards Brigade. A cousin, Alan Shutler, served in No.2 (Grenadier Guards) Company as part of 3rd Battalion, Welsh Guards, the same battalion as Gareth Scanlon's great grandfathers. Alan lies in the Commonwealth War

Graves Cemetery at Indicatore, near Arezzo, killed in action on 8 August 1944 during the advance towards Florence.

The Allied Armies used tactics learned from hard experience and from other theatres and there were attempts at innovation, despite the hard slog and limited resources. Italy did see the effective deployment of air power, armour and artillery, despite some early failures and the severe constraints listed above.

Gareth Scanlon has put together a detailed study of the 6th Armoured Division. He presents not only a family history, but also a comprehensive analysis of the uniforms, the innovative use of camouflage clothing and the adaptation of the Guards and Rifle regiments of the Division to the climate, terrain and vegetation of central Italy during the summer of 1944. The result of many years of detailed research and painstaking acquisition of the uniforms and other accoutrements worn by the guardsmen and riflemen, *Camouflaged Fist* provides a deep analysis of their origins, sources and modifications.

This book makes a significant contribution to our knowledge of the war in Italy from a barely tapped but fruitful direction for what is often portrayed as a dull, unimaginative and colourless campaign.

Dr Nigel Warwick
Corps Historian Royal Air Force Regiment
Military & Air Power Historian

Preface

Having been born in 1981, I am of the pre-computer game, Airfix generation and owe my obsession with modern history to my Dad, Mark Scanlon. This transfer of interest principally came from the time we spent together building scale models of aircraft and vehicles from the Second World War. This was then augmented by frequent family holidays to France which naturally included obligatory visits to museums across Normandy and the Atlantic Coast. As a child I read widely, and vividly recall a red cover history book printed in 1957 which gave an overview of the Second World War in some seven pages[2] – I still have it today and it is a prized possession. As a teenager my interest and studies intensified during my school years and as soon as I was able to drive I was to be found spending many a summer visiting the battlefields of Normandy and began collecting artefacts from the conflict. I went on to study towards a BA (Hons) degree at the University of Liverpool but, regrettably, I did not complete my studies.

During my youth, the veterans of the Second World War were gentlemen in their seventies, but very much a part of the fabric of life in West Wales, where I grew up. One of those was my great grandfather, who I was lucky to know into early adulthood. While being imposing in stature, he was quite possibly the gentlest man I have ever met. I recall as a small child eating home baked cakes at his kitchen side table as he sat smiling and chuckling. I also remember his extensive garden and wonderful collection of plants, the cuttings of which continue to survive within my parents' garden today, all created and nurtured by his skilled hand. He was a model great grandfather; kind, soft and warm. I knew as a child that *Dadcu* (*Dad-ki* Welsh for grandfather, also interchangeable with great grandfather) was in the war and I often asked him about his war years. His usual reply to any question came in the Welsh language with an accompanying chuckle – the answer to whatever was asked was almost always swerved. As I got older, my questions became more probing and his answers became more detailed. Despite Dadcu's gentle and warm nature, my journey of discovery has led me to know that he often found himself at the very sharpest end of the war; fighting the enemy at close quarters, often hand-to-hand. If only I had known then, while he was alive, what I know now, my questions to him would be very different. To that end, as many of us have done, I have tried to improve my understanding of this chapter of his life and of his individual contribution to the collective defeat of fascism in Europe.

My Dadcu was 2733859 David Glyndwr Spowart, a professional soldier who joined the Welsh Guards in 1934. His first taste of active service came 6 years later on 22 May 1940 with 2nd Battalion Welsh Guards as a part of 20th Guards Brigade. He disembarked from a merchant ship at Boulogne in an ill-fated attempt to reinforce the garrison of that vital port. Two days later, he and the remainder of the Guards were hurriedly re-embarked and returned to Britain, they had suffered heavy casualties, especially in prisoners.

On 24 October 1941, the holding battalion for accepting new, post-Dunkirk Welsh Guards recruits was changed to become a third infantry battalion.[3] He was transferred to this new battalion as a lance corporal on 20 January 1943, likely on account of the need to form a nucleus of experienced Non-Commissioned Officers. This, previously untested battalion was sent to join the 1st Army in Tunisia. Here 3rd Battalion Welsh Guards joined 1st Guards Brigade of 6th *Mailed Fist* Armoured Division in March 1943. In time, this Brigade would become known as 'The Plumbers' on account of it always being called in to plug a hole.[4]'

From TNA, WO 417/60[5]

On 8 May 1943, during an assault on a hill near Hammam Lif in Tunisia, Dadcu (then a Lance Sergeant) was wounded in the chest and thigh by a mortar shell as his company advanced across open ground under heavy fire.

Following the collapse of Axis resistance in Tunisia in May 1943, 6th Armoured Division remained in the Mediterranean Theatre. The invasion of the Italian mainland occurred during September 1943 but the campaign was slowing due to the harsh winter, and stiffening enemy resistance. The 1st Guards Brigade was temporarily detached from 6th Armoured Division and sent to Italy in February 1944. The Brigade was immediately thrust into action in extreme winter conditions in the Aurunci Mountains, north-west of Naples. The challenging arid and rocky terrain, awful weather and the skilled and determined resistance from the enemy was to become a continuing theme throughout his war in Italy. As a 'D-Day Dodger', Dadcu remained with 1st Guards Brigade throughout the Italian campaign and ended the war in Austria in May 1945.

He spent 552 days in active combat zones; three days at Boulogne in 1940, 97 days in Tunisia and 452 in Italy. During his time with the 2nd and 3rd Battalions he was to participate in actions which resulted in 15 battle honours being awarded:

> Boulogne 1940, Fondouk, Djebel el Rhorab, Tunis, Hammam Lif, North Africa 1943, Monte Ornito, Liri Valley, Monte Piccolo, Capture of Perugia, Arezzo, Advance to Florence, Gothic Line, Monte Battaglia and Italy 1944–45.

PREFACE

Philip Brutton, an officer who served in 8 Platoon of 3rd Company, 3rd Battalion Welsh Guards, remarked in the closing lines of his account:

> The 3rd Battalion Welsh Guards left for North Africa on 5 February, 1943, and returned to Great Britain on 18 August 1945. One thousand men went out; there were one thousand casualties; and one thousand men came back.[6]

This represented a 100 percent casualty rate; Italy bled the infantry away. As a Foot Guard, and even more so as an NCO, it was a miracle that he survived – they did a lot of hill fighting and that required an awful lot of leadership. The Commonwealth War Graves Commission recorded 202 dead for the battalion during the war.

The circular from Lieutenant Colonel Rose Price D.S.O, Commanding Officer 3rd Battalion Welsh Guards dated 3 May 1945 further explains Brutton's statement. It was found within a grouping of effects to a Lance Corporal (and later Sergeant) G. White owned by the author.

The 3rd Battalion Welsh Guards left 6th Armoured Division in Austria during July 1945. At the farewell speech, General McCreery said that they had been, 'one of the most efficient battalions in Eighth Army.'[7]

The genesis of this work is principally founded upon me stumbling across a single high-resolution photograph, one that I had seen many times before, albeit poorly reproduced. This image (as shown on the cover and in more detail later) has enabled me to positively identify *Dadcu* in full battle order with his section – he is fourth from left, bare headed.

Following the initial dumbfounded realisation of the incredible odds in uncovering an image of my *Dadcu*, particularly of him in the field, I became curious about the non-standard clothing he and his section were wearing. Readers of this will likely recognise the standard image of the World War Two Tommy neatly turned out in battledress and pack, however, in this photograph that was not the case; the men are wearing khaki U.S. Army Enlisted Man's shirts, denim battledress trousers, helmets covered in Indian pattern nets and, most peculiarly, enemy Pattern M1929 Italian *Telo Mimetico* camouflage smocks. A blend of uniform from four countries!

The importance of the smocks to the identity of 3rd Battalion of the Welsh Guards was such that they featured in a Regimental Christmas Card (below) drawn by 2733698 Lance Sergeant G. S. Murrell. Incidentally, the Lance Sergeant provided many of the illustrations for Major L. F. Ellis's regimental history, *Welsh Guards at War* (see bibliography). It is inscribed to the rear in both English and Welsh with: 'Christmas 1944, *Nadolig Llawen A Blwyddyn Newydd Dda*, With Best Wishes For Christmas And The New Year From.'

These smocks spiked my interest, and my quest to learn as much about them as I possibly could, culminated in this book.

As a final twist, while this book was undergoing pre-publication checks, I received another piece of staggering information. In late December 2023, the husband of my great aunt sadly passed away at his home in South Africa. Following his passing my family discovered two newspaper clippings of obituaries to another great grandfather, Samuel Davies. Astoundingly, the clippings confirm that he also fought in the Italian campaign with 3rd

CAMOUFLAGED FIST

SPECIAL ORDER OF THE DAY
Being the address given to the Bn on 3rd May 1945 by the Commanding Officer.

Officers, warrant officers, non-commissioned officers and Guardsmen of the 3rd Battalion WELSH GUARDS - in which I include most particularly our medical officer, our padre, our Brigade signal detachment, our TCV Platoon and the REME personnel attached to us.

The GERMAN armies in ITALY have surrendered unconditionally to Field Marshal ALEXANDER and it can only be a matter of days before they surrender unconditionally in GERMANY.

I thought it right that we should all meet together here on this great day and mark the occasion and that I should say a word.

I think our hearts are very full. In mine I find equal measure of thankfulness and pride. Profound thankfulness that this business is now ended and tremendous and proper pride in this great Battalion and in all that it has done.

FONDOUK - HAMMAMLIF - CERASOLA - MONTE PURGATORIO - MONTE GRANDE - MONTE PICCOLO - CASSINO - PERUGIA - MONTE BATTAGLIA - MONTE VERRO and the crossing of the River PO.

Today we are 820 strong.

Almost exactly 1000 Guardsmen sailed from ENGLAND on 5th February 1943 and since then almost exactly 1000 more have come to us.

Of those who sailed that day, there are 389 with us now - but we are NOT all here and we think of those in hospitals in this country and in ENGLAND, of those doing jobs in this country and of those at the IRTD and we think of all those from Commanding Officer downwards - if I may use the word - who gave much in the construction, shaping, training and fighting of this Battalion. We think of those who may still be prisoners - and there were only 45 of these and of those most particularly to the number of 184 who gave all; and perhaps a special thought for the relatives of 6782 Guardsman MORRIS of the Support Company, who alone in these last battles has died, as the result of an accident.

And now, and I hope without marring the occasion and because I have not had an opportunity of speaking to you as a whole since I took command 12 days ago, I am going to strike a more personal note.

Some of you may not know that two of the original companies of this Battalion were number 6 holding company and number 7 holding company and that I was the first company commander of number 6 and that your second in command, Major GRESHAM was the first company commander of number 7. These two companies later became our present number 3 and 4 companies and there are present in these companies and elsewhere in the Battalion some of those original men.

Since those days, I have often gone absent from the Battalion but our ways have often lain close together and our business has always been the same so that it is not possible for me to describe my own great happiness in being given the honour of leading this Battalion in its final battles and bringing it safely home to port.

I think the soldierly quality which has always appealed to me most is dash.

At that late stage of the war, it was harder for us all to take risks; but each day, one saw what one knew one would see; each and every one of you showing unmistakably that you were members of this most gallant Battalion.

It may have its equals, and I think we know of two. It has no superior in the Brigade of Guards.

R C Rose Price

Lt.Col.
Officer Commanding,
3rd Bn Welsh Guards.

CONEGLIANO.
ITALY.
3 May 45.

PREFACE

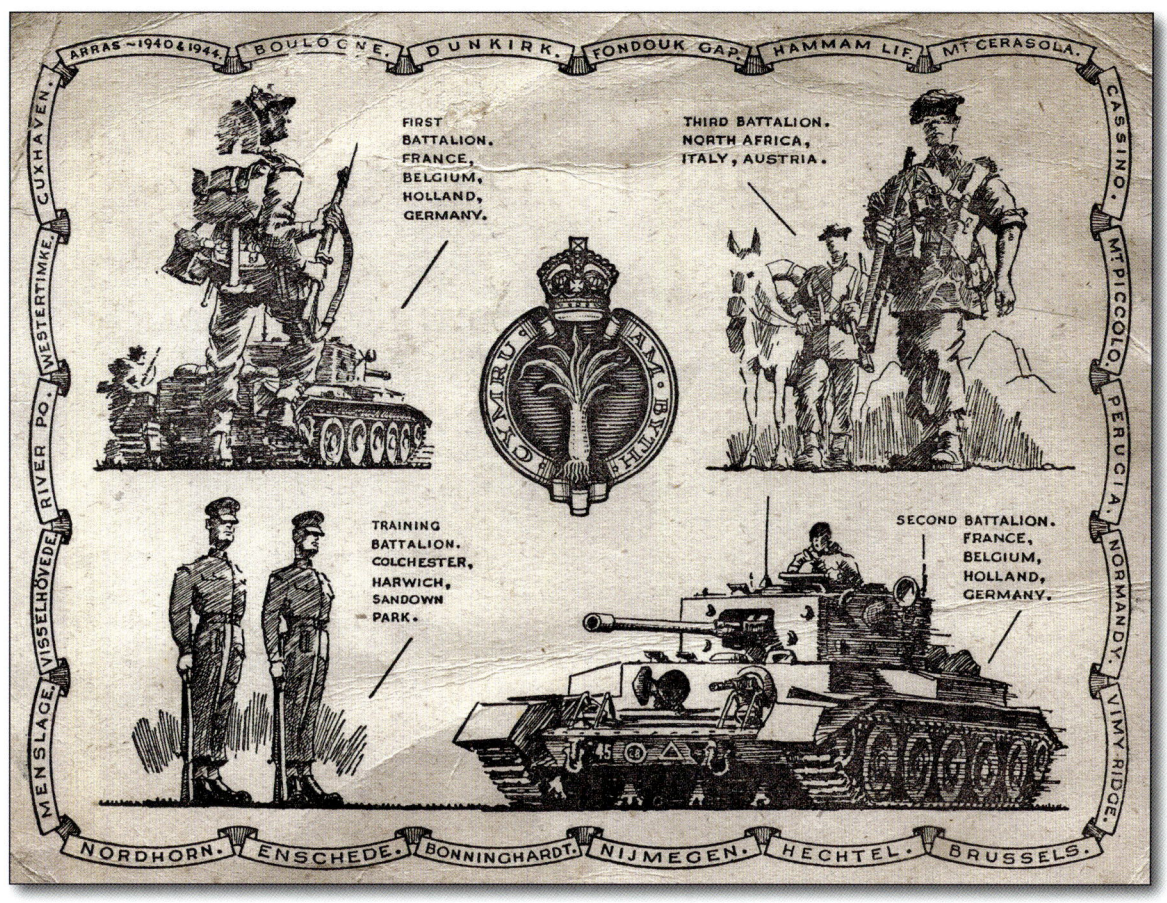

(The author is grateful to Tom Sellen for donating this item to the collection)

Battalion Welsh Guards too. Unfortunately, I was never able to meet Sam as he passed away nine years before I was born, although my mother loved him dearly and often recounts his gentle nature.

Samuel Davies spent the majority of his life living within the adjacent village to that of my other great grandfather Glyn, and it is beyond doubt that they would have known each other given the close-knit community of the Quarter Bach area of Carmarthenshire in South-West Wales. Given that they both survived the Italian campaign, and the high casualty rates already mentioned, it is distinctly probable that they would have known each other within the Welsh Guards; they may have even directly served together.

I have no photographs of Sam from the war years as yet and remain hopeful that some will be located in the future. I cannot help but wonder whether he is present in any of the photographs that I already own of the Welsh Guards in Italy that are reproduced throughout this book, or indeed in those also containing my other great grandfather Glyn.

I have requested his Service Record to learn more, but regrettably it could take several months for it to be returned and consequently it is unavailable as this book goes to press and any details contained within it will thus, sadly not feature within this title.

Acknowledgements

This book would not have been possible without several people whom I would like to express my thanks to here:

I am grateful to the friendship of Tom Sellen, who has provided endless support and guidance from his extensive knowledge and experience as a battlefield tour guide. Tom was also kind enough to model in original contemporary uniform and equipment for the images in the colour plates. Similarly, my brother-in-law Alex Summerbell and local historian Scott James also modelled for photographs, and I am very grateful to the latter given his family circumstances at that time.

My grateful thanks to Orazio Spampinato and Daniele Piselli, himself an author, for making the camouflage smocks within their own collections available to photograph and for their continued pooling and sharing of knowledge and information. Thanks also to Emanuele Moretti for introducing me to Orazio and Daniele, without that crucial connection, the comparisons of surviving examples contained within this title would never have been possible. My good friend, Riccardo Bizzaro, an avid 1st Guards Brigade historian, collector and living history practitioner has provided valuable insight into the Italian climate, landscape and the use of blanco by the brigade, amongst a wealth of other useful information.

Drs Nigel Warwick and Adam Robson, again both celebrated authors themselves, have been instrumental in providing additional information, advice, guidance and reading lists to assist my research. I also wish to thank Gary Tankard who has copied and supplied multiple documents from a variety of sources held at the National Archives in Kew, London. Neil Powell of www.battlefieldhistorian.com has also gone to great efforts to make available previously unseen and unpublished wartime photographs contained within this title that bring visual context to the narrative.

I also owe gratitude to Przemysław Świderek and Steve Lawrence who assisted me in locating the smock, now held in my own collection, and to John Bown for agreeing to part with it. Stephen Kiddle of Pegasus Militaria was also a key contributor in providing advice and guidance leading up to the acquisition of my original example. I am also extremely grateful to the wife of my brother-in-law, Athina Summerbell, who painstakingly made an exact replica of my own smock which significantly enhanced my understanding of how these were fabricated.

ACKNOWLEDGEMENTS

A special mention to my friend and colleague Peter Roderick for all of his encouragement as well. My parents, Heather and Mark, for their lifelong support, nurturing and unwavering belief. My brother Rhodri, who is writing a book regarding another great grandfather who fought and was captured at the Battle of Audregnies near Mons in 1914, for his enthusiasm in cheering the project on and for proof reading multiple drafts of this book.

Finally, and most crucially, I will be forever indebted to my darling wife Rachel and my son Henry, not only for enduring my various obsessions which have enabled this book to become a reality, but for the time to create it to the detriment of other things.

Gareth Scanlon
Ammanford
March 2024

Introduction

> Italy was an infantryman's war, a gritty blend of ancient and modern warfare. A second front, fought by 'D-Day Dodgers'; since forgotten and overshadowed by the events of Normandy and North-West Europe.[8]

Churchill once told Stalin that the Mediterranean was the 'soft underbelly of Europe.' U.S. Lieutenant General Mark Clark soon coined the phrase, to the contrary, that Italy was 'one tough gut' and it certainly was.

It was hoped that the invasion of Italy would knock the country out of the war, secure new airfields to further intensify the strategic bombing campaign and enable the Allied Armies to enter Austria and from thence into the heart of Germany. It would also tie down German divisions and draw in reserves away from North-West Europe and the Eastern Front, the latter meeting demands from Stalin to continue the fight on the second front. The Allies were ill prepared for Italy's diverse climate and geography and they quickly discovered it did not play to their strengths as a highly mechanised and manoeuvrable army. Conversely, the Germans skilfully waged a war of denial and attrition, fighting a slow and tenacious retreat to prepared lines of defence using the mountainous terrain and multiple rivers to inflict maximum delay and destruction of the Allies. The withdrawal of experienced Allied divisions in preparation for D-Day further exacerbated the challenges faced. This forced the Allied Armies in Italy to continually develop, innovate and change to suit the situation and environment that presented.

To that end, this book is intended to establish the who, what, why, where, when and how surrounding the use of these innovative non-standard camouflage smocks by the infantry brigades of 6th Armoured Division. It will also use previously unpublished period photographs to outline the drivers for change, and set out when and where the smocks were used, and establish who made them and how.

There has been a great deal written about the uniforms and equipment used by British Forces in North-West Europe, but comparatively very little for on what was used in Italy, which is surprising given the broader, and arguably more interesting, spectrum of items used there.

The use of camouflage clothing by the British Army during the Second World War was predominantly confined to that issued to special forces. This included the 'Airborne Smock, Denison, Camouflage' (often shortened simply to Denison smock) used by Airborne and Commando units or to those operating in particular environments, for example in snow. This was later augmented by a more widespread issue of the 'Smock, Windproof, Camouflage' to regular infantry units from 1943 onwards. For most infantrymen personal concealment and camouflage equipment was limited to the use of a variety of helmet nets, blanco (a compound mixed with water used to colour webbing), early war camouflage capes, blackening of skin and the personal net (often referred to as the face veil).

It is interesting that the specific need for a garment offering a solution to a tactical problem was such, that it was produced in an organised and systematic way by a Royal Army Ordnance Corps factory, in theatre, despite not being an official War Department issue item. Notwithstanding this official manufacture, there was very limited reliable information immediately available regarding this garment.

This sparked the author's thirst for more information which, in turn, instigated a period of deep and painstaking research into eyewitness testimony, accounts, unit histories, and the examination of War Diaries to battalion level as well as other archival research and an engagement with subject matter experts.

The author has inevitably focused much of his studies on the Battalions of the 'drippings'[9] (Cockney rhyming slang – Drippings and Lard = Guards) that made up 1st Guards Brigade, namely 3rd Battalion Grenadier Guards, 2nd Battalion Coldstream Guards and 3rd Battalion Welsh Guards. This was then naturally extended to include the Rifle Battalions which formed the 61st Infantry Brigade which joined 6th Armoured Division in late May 1944. This additional infantry brigade reflected the quickly changing role and requirements of an armoured division fighting the war in Italy. It consisted of the 2nd, 7th and 10th Battalions of The Rifle Brigade, Prince Consort's Own.

There have been numerous frustrations, challenges and setbacks along the way, mainly attributed to consuming vast amounts of what initially appeared promising written material often to find, disappointingly, no references to the garment whatsoever. This niche research project has however enabled this book to become a reality, and the author sincerely hopes that it will fill a gap in the knowledge of and narrative around these garments.

In investigating the subject, the author was also extremely lucky to acquire an original smock, one of only a handful of known British examples to survive the war. Consequently, this has enabled the production of detailed photographs of the garment in addition to those of two other surviving examples cherished in private collections in Italy. It has also allowed several photographs to be taken to replicate accounts, photographs and narratives found by the author during the research to bring colour visualisation to the past. Whilst this publication will likely be of interest and assistance to both military collectors, scale modellers and historians alike, it may also support the identification and authentication of any further surviving examples of this rare garment that may come to light.

The author also wishes to outline to the reader *what this book isn't*. There are a plethora of outstanding books available which tell the story of the Italian campaign of World War II, often in great depth and covering strategic, tactical and operational aspects from the perspectives of all belligerents. Similarly, there are numerous excellent titles detailing the wartime exploits of 6th Armoured Division. This book also does not offer an in-depth account of the wide variety of *Telo Mimetico* colourings, patterns and garments used by British, Italian, German and other forces during the Second World War nor that of official War Department issue uniform. Any accounts on these matters are used to set the scene only in the context of the use of the camouflage smock.

The book will assume the reader has some pre-existing knowledge of the campaign and will likely appeal to those already possessing a strong interest in the Italian campaign. Therefore, to cover such matters here would be both unnecessary and superfluous. In saying that, the author hopes that this book may bring a new spotlight on, and interest in, the men that served in the Italian campaign, particularly since more Allied servicemen from the Second World War are buried on Italian soil than that of North-West Europe.

These camouflage smocks were also used by other British units during the campaign, notably:

- 5th Battalion Royal West Kents, 21st Indian Infantry Brigade, 8th Indian Division,
- 1st Battalion Royal Fusiliers, 17th Indian Infantry Brigade, 8th Indian Division,
- 3rd Battalion Coldstream Guards, 24th Guards Brigade, 6th South African Armoured Division, and
- 1st Battalion Scots Guards, 24th Guards Brigade, 6th South African Armoured Division.

They were also used by other Commonwealth and Allied units, although the garments were notably different to those used by the British in terms of size and construction:

- New Zealand 24th Infantry Battalion, 6th NZ Infantry Brigade, 2nd NZ Division,
- Various units of 2nd Polish Corps.

Use by the above listed units falls outside the scope of this study but is subject to further and ongoing research.

Those books, accounts and documents that have proved most useful have been included in the bibliography.

All modern photographs of maps, pamphlets, uniform and items of equipment are from the author's personal collection unless otherwise stipulated.

Chapter 1

Italy: Geography & Climate and Impact on the Campaign

The thousand mile long Italian Peninsula has been of strategic importance for millennia in holding a prominent location at the crossroads of the European, African and Asian continents. Surrounded by the Mediterranean Sea on three sides, the Alps in the north act as a natural barrier separating Italy from its neighbours. The 800 mile virtually impenetrable Apennine Mountain Range with its peaks and spurs forms the spine of the country stretching from Lombardy in the north to the tip of the 'toe of Italy'. Descending from these mountains is a complex network of valleys and rivers which flow from the peaks to the Mediterranean Sea on both sides, each forming individual natural barriers. The rugged terrain, mountainous regions, and vast river networks posed significant challenges for the Allied advance to the north and shaped the strategic course of the campaign.

This situation was further frustrated by the rarity of the metalled roads that are required by mechanised armies. All of this forced the Allies to initially proceed along narrow cordons on the east and west coasts. These geographic and infrastructural features reduced the efficiency of supply lines presenting further complications in the transportation of troops, equipment and supplies which would hamper the speed and progress of all Allied operations.

To compound matters further, Field Marshal Kesselring's defence of Italy in 1943/44 was to be by prosecuting a war of denial and attrition and a slow retreat to prepared defensive positions. Kesselring was a talented commander and had already demonstrated his skill in conducting defensive operations in retreat. Following the invasion of Sicily in July 1943, he was able to extricate most of his forces during Operation *Lehrgang*, a mini Dunkirk-like evacuation back to the Italian mainland via the Straights of Messina. He turned the Apennine Mountains into a veritable 800 mile obstacle course and formed numerous defensive lines of interlocking positions. These were often located on both the rear and front crests of hills which exploited every twist in the terrain to the advantage of the defender. In many cases these lines were some 10 miles deep and were both hard and costly to breach. Occupation of the mountains gave the Germans excellent observation positions which also ensured that Allied forces were almost always overlooked.

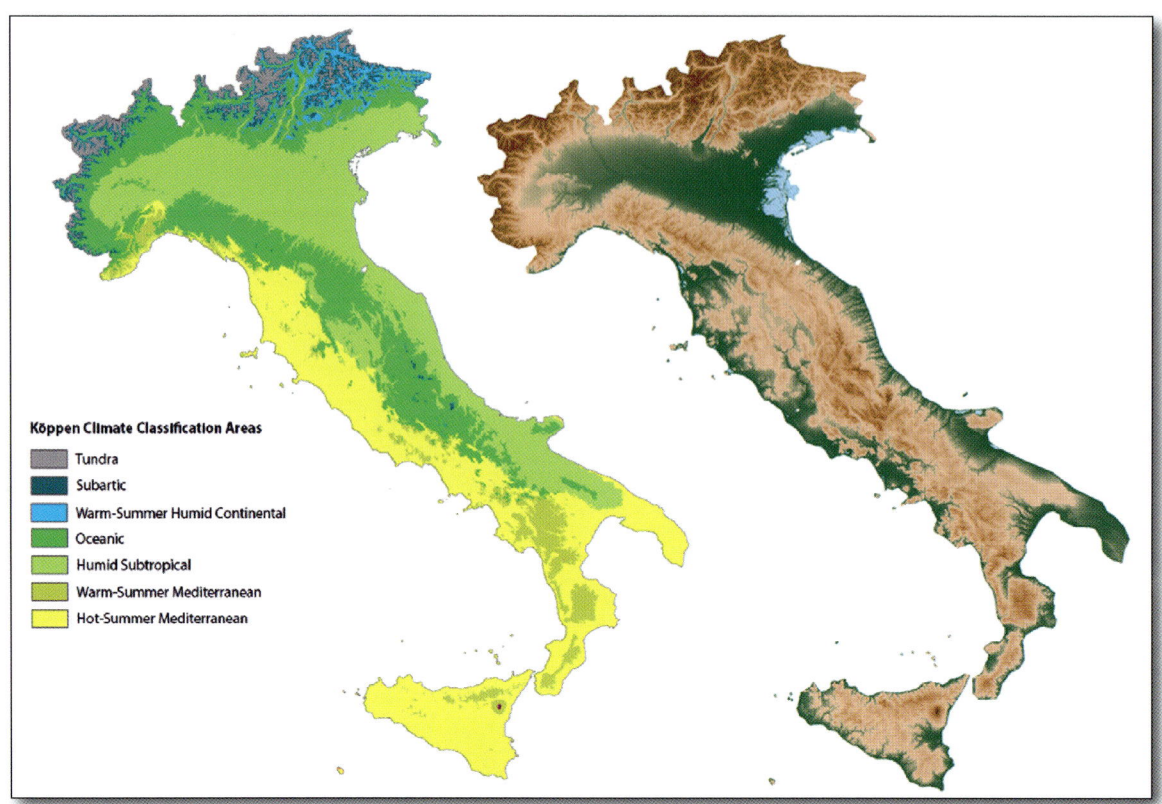

Köppen Climate Classification
& Topographic Maps of Italy.[10]

The Germans used millions of mines, booby traps and road blocks to frustrate the use of the few available roads, passes and valleys, all of which further slowed any advance. They then covered these areas with thinly manned concealed positions with interlocking fields of machine gun fire and expertly operated mortars, which often came into action within a minute of the onset of any engagement. The Germans breached river banks and blew bridges then concentrated their destruction on the resultant congested build-up of troops, vehicles and supplies at crossing points, in order to inflict maximum damage. The German defensive tactic was to continually engage the Allies under fire and use troops occupying the reverse slopes of mountains, safe from Allied artillery, to swiftly counter-attack with additional fire before withdrawing to the next obstacle. This tactic reduced the effectiveness of Allied artillery, another of the Allies' key strengths, by forcing the need to fire at high angles to clear the mountain tops to engage the enemy occupying the reverse slopes.

It could be said that the mountain ranges and geography of Italy became Kesselring's principal ally following the Italian capitulation on 8 September 1943 and the almost immediate disarmament of their forces thereafter under Operation *Achse*.

ITALY: GEOGRAPHY & CLIMATE AND IMPACT ON THE CAMPAIGN

A German Observation Team *Vorgeschobener Beobachter*, Italy 1944.

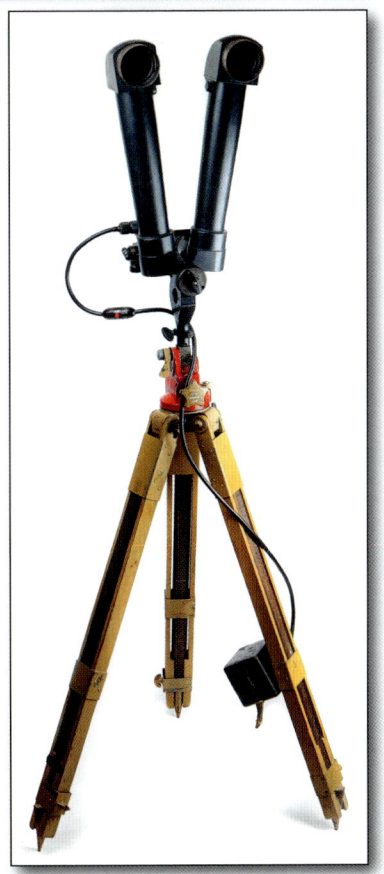

A German *Scherenfernrohr 14 (S.F.14)* 10x50 periscope binocular mounted upon a late war *Gestell 41* tripod complete with reticule light, cable and battery box. This system was comprised of a high acuity 10x magnification optical device mounted on a sturdy and fully adjustable tripod. This quality optic complete with reticule lighting, enabled an accurate and reasonably portable range finding and observation system fit for all lighting and weather conditions. Its periscope-like design served two purposes; firstly, the ability to be deployed from cover protecting the observation crew while also making it extremely difficult to detect and spot. Secondly, the length of the tubes combined with the 'V-shaped' splay function greatly accentuates a three dimensional image via the parallax effect which improved the viewer's depth perception, thus increasing the accuracy of range finding. It was through systems such as these, in addition to other high acuity hand held binoculars, that the Allies were kept under constant observation and accurate fire as they advanced along the peninsula.

Sapper A. G. Taylor disarming booby traps at Diacceto, east of Florence on 21 August 1944. The doll in the ruins was found to be attached to the pull-igniter of a teller mine (an anti-vehicle mine). Note the Mailed Fist formation sign worn on the epaulettes of his khaki drill shirt and the use of two helmet nets.[11]

Kesselring's strategy, in combination with the geography, denied the Allies the ability to bring to bear their strengths of firepower, materiel and mobility. This likely represented a severe shock to the system for those Allied commanders who had fought in the wide expanses of the Western Desert just months prior. Notwithstanding the need for a port, the political objective in occupying Rome, the requirement to seize valuable airfields near Foggia and Salerno being the most northerly beachhead that could sustain an amphibious landing while retaining vital air cover; many would question the wisdom of invading Italy from the south!

Italy was an infantryman's war. Fighting was hilltop to hilltop, building to building and often at close range, hand-to-hand combat was commonplace. Infantrymen carried everything they needed on their backs, especially water, bullets and hand grenades – and Italy is vertical, it is akin to attacking a staircase with layers of defences built up and up with every step.

ITALY: GEOGRAPHY & CLIMATE AND IMPACT ON THE CAMPAIGN

Sapper M. J. Coyne of 625 Field Squadron removing a German Egg Grenade from a booby-trapped fruit tree. Orchards were frequently booby-trapped to injure Allied troops looking to supplement their rations.[12]

Rifleman Alex Bowlby of 2nd Rifle Battalion, 61st Brigade recounts an order issued in the Liri Valley in late May 1944:

> Each rifleman will carry a pick or shovel, two hundred rounds of ammo, two grenades, and four Bren gun magazines. Steel helmets will be worn. So will greatcoats – in bandolier style. Small packs, gas capes and entrenching tools will be carried in the usual way.[13]

Those unfortunate men who were unlucky enough to be wounded while fighting in the hills often had to be carried back several miles to reach full medical aid, or even to a point at which they could be transferred to a vehicle. It was a gritty slog, on foot, against stubborn and skilled defenders with a unique blend of ancient and modern warfare.

Italy's geographical features and its position inevitably shapes its extremely diverse climate and environments. Climate conditions on the coast are very different from those in the interior and conditions in the north are very different to those in the south. In terms of landscape, the south is quintessentially Mediterranean with dusty rocky hills, sand, sparse vegetation and cacti. In stark contrast to this, both Umbria and Tuscany feature green rolling hills, lush valleys, olive groves, vineyards and cypress lined roads. In further contrast, the Po Valley is flat with grass hills, dominated by the Alps to the north.

During the winter months higher altitudes are cold, wet, and often snowy whereas coastal regions and lowland valleys have mild winters and dry hot summers. Allied to that, daily temperatures can vary by up to 20 degrees Celsius across the country over any given day.

Environments, climates and landscapes also change dramatically within short travelling distances. For example, many will be acquainted with images taken during the Battle of Cassino and its arid and rocky environment for it to give way, within a short distance, to lush, green and fertile countryside.

Allied planners seriously misjudged, and were completely unprepared for, the Italian climate and as a result the infantrymen lived at the mercy of ice, snow, rain, mud and tropical heat. In most cases the weather was a far cry from the sunny pictures of Italy that the men expected. The blizzards, snow thaws and rain resulted in paths, and the already inadequate road system, turning to thick mud, photographs of which were more akin to those of the Eastern Front in Russia than Italy. Cold trauma injuries such as frostbite and exposure were common as were other injuries more associated with World War One, such as trench foot. All of this played into the hands of the defender, with the further advantage that poor weather and low cloud covers hampered Allied observation from the air. Motor vehicles became more of a hindrance than a help, and this necessitated the replacement of vehicles with more primitive sources of transport such as mules and their accompanying, often Italian, muleteers to deliver supplies of food, fuel and other items of necessary equipment for the waging of war. A division required more than 1600 mules to adequately support it. Philip Brutton recounted that:

> In terms of country over which the 3rd Battalion [Welsh Guards] fought, the contrasts were extreme: …. the extreme cold and rock-strewn exposure of Monte Ornito [and Creasola, Aurunci Mountains]; the total desolation of Cassino; the hot, dusty battles of the Liri Valley, permeated with the stench of death; …. winter lines held on mountain tops which, to reach, took eight hours of motor transport and then almost as many on foot to the front; the mule trains and the mud; the evacuation of casualties and the problems of supply.[14]

This unending battlefield with its ever-shifting, and arguably multiple fronts, exacerbated by the German strategy and diverse climate, forced the Allies to evolve and innovate to meet the circumstances and challenges being faced.

ITALY: GEOGRAPHY & CLIMATE AND IMPACT ON THE CAMPAIGN

MULE RIDING IS TRICKY even without an umbrella. A Fifth Army "jockey."

A magazine cutting retained from within the effects of Lance Corporal G. White and now in the collection of the author. Given the deliberate act of removing it from the magazine one can only presume that this was done to maintain the memory of the mules and muleteers of the division, thus indicating their importance to the men.

Soldiers of the Allied Armies in Italy

Throughout the past winter you have fought hard and valiantly and killed many Germans. Perhaps you are disappointed that we have not been able to advance faster and farther, but I and those who know, realize full well how magnificently you have fought amongst these almost insurmountable obstacles of rocky, trackless mountains, deep in snow, and in valleys blocked by rivers and mud, against a stubborn foe.

The results of these past months may not appear spectacular, but you have drawn into Italy and mauled many of the enemy's best divisions which he badly needed to stem the advance of the Russian Armies in the East. Hitler has admitted that his defeats in the East were largely due to the bitterness of the fighting and his losses in Italy. This, in itself, is a great achievement and you may well be as proud of yourselves as I am of you. You have gained the admiration of the world and the gratitude of our Russian Allies.

Today the bad times are behind us and tomorrow we can see victory ahead. Under the ever increasing blows of the air forces of the United Nations, which are mounting every day in intensity, the German war machine is beginning to crumble. The Allied armed forces are now assembling for the final battles on sea, on land, and in the air to crush the enemy once and for all. From the East and the West, from the North and the South, blows are about to fall which will result in the final destruction of the Nazis and bring freedom once again to Europe, and hasten peace for us all. To us in Italy, has been given the honour to strike the first blow.

We are going to destroy the German Armies in Italy. The fighting will be hard, bitter, and perhaps long, but you are warriors and soldiers of the highest order, who for more than a year have known only victory. You have courage, determination and skill. You will be supported by overwhelming air forces, and in guns and tanks we far outnumber the Germans. No Armies have ever entered battle before with a more just and righteous cause.

So with God's help and blessing, we take the field—confident of victory.

H.R. Alexander

General,
Commander - in - Chief,
Allied Armies in Italy

May, 1944

General Alexander, in a 'circular' to his troops in May 1944, accounts for the scale of the difficulties faced in the campaign.

ITALY: GEOGRAPHY & CLIMATE AND IMPACT ON THE CAMPAIGN

The deprivations and hardships faced by the men were captured in true British comedic style through the Two Types cartoon characters. These were created by John 'Jon' Jones, a Welshman from Llandrindod Wells, and was popular throughout the Mediterranean Theatre in newspapers and pamphlets. These images are taken from a popular booklet produced by the British Army Newspaper Unit Central Mediterranean Forces 'for the fighting men of all ranks in theatre.' It was distributed by the Directorate of Army Welfare Services, Allied Forces Headquarters, and cost 20 lire.

Riflemen of 61st Brigade cross the River Melfa on 25 May 1944 near Pontecorvo, Liri Valley. Note the terrain encountered and the potential havoc and destruction that German artillery could cause on the concentration of troops and vehicles at sites of blown bridges as referenced earlier. (Photograph courtesy of Neil Powell, www.battlefieldhistorian.com)

Four Sherman tanks of the Derbyshire Yeomanry were able to cross the bridge before an M10 of 72nd Anti-tank Regiment was hit by an anti-tank shell and burst into flames. As the bridge was wooden it burned as well. One of the four Shermans was also destroyed before 10th Rifle Battalion were able to cross the bridge to provide infantry support some seven hours later.[15]

Note how the banks have been modified to enable vehicles to ford the Melfa to the left and right of the bridge. These modifications were likely created by the bulldozers of 625 Field Squadron, Royal Engineers, 6th Armoured Division who were at that time under command of the Derbyshire Yeomanry.[16]

ITALY: GEOGRAPHY & CLIMATE AND IMPACT ON THE CAMPAIGN

Note the face veil being carried 'bandolier style' over the shoulder of the rifleman in the extreme left foreground and the use of utility pouches to carry extra ammunition by many of the men. Also note that most are wearing denim battledress.

Also note the Mailed Fist 6th Armoured Division formation signs on the epaulettes of the khaki drill shirt worn by the rifleman pushing the motorcycle to the right. Photograph courtesy of Neil Powell, www.battlefieldhistorian.com.

An additional view of the same scene showing an alternative angle of the knocked out M10. (Photograph courtesy of Neil Powell, www.battlefieldhistorian.com) Note also the tubular ford laid by the engineers. The photograph below was the first taken in the series. The fourth man back in the column in this photograph is seen in the right foreground of the one above. The third man carrying the Bren gun over his shoulder can be seen just out of shot on the far left also. (Photograph courtesy of Neil Powell, www.battlefieldhistorian.com)

Chapter 2

6th Armoured Division: Infantry Brigade Composition

Following the defeat of Axis Forces in Tunisia on 14 May 1943 6th Armoured Division underwent a period of retraining and reorganisation in Algeria. Elements of the division arrived in Italy in early January 1944 starting with the 16th/5th Lancers who were temporarily attached to 23rd Armoured Brigade from 9 January to 29 March 1944. However, it was not the division's armour that Alexander required but its infantry and artillery. To that end, on 5 February 1944 1st Guards Brigade disembarked from the *Ville d'Oran* at Naples harbour where it too was temporarily detached from the 6th Armoured Division.

Alexander was quick to realise that the inadequate road infrastructure and geography meant there was little, 'scope for Armoured Divisions as such in Italy.'[17] 6th Armoured Division very nearly became dissolved before it had even set foot on Italian soil.

On 13 January 1944 Alexander sent a memo to AFHQ, which was responsible for all Allied operational forces in the Me diterranean Theatre. The three-page memo made several requests and recommendations including amongst other things, the formation of a Guards Infantry Division:

1. I have given careful consideration to the employment of armoured formations in future operations in Italy, and to the number of armoured divisions and independent armoured or tank brigades I am likely to require …

2. Experience up-to-date has shown that there is little scope for armoured Divisions as such in ITALY. The enclosed and mountainous nature of the country and the difficulty of deploying off the roads has restricted the employment of tanks to operations in close cooperation with infantry, for which tank brigades are best suited. The country between the ALBEGIIO (*sic*) and ARNO rivers may be found to offer more scope for armoured divisions, but even if that proves to be the case I think that two armoured divisions are the most I am likely able to employ simultaneously. The same remark applies to operations in the valley of the PO. On the other hand a minimum scale of one regiment of tanks will, I consider be required for close cooperation with each infantry division.

…

4. 1 and 6 Brit Armd Divs, have been in NORTH AFRICA since the end of the TUNISIAN campaign, and can hardly be improving in morale or efficiency through being kept so long out of battle. I understand that 1 Armd Div is not required in the UK and I therefore suggest that the following action be taken to make the best use of this very valuable manpower: -
    (a) The infantry brigades of 1 and 6 Armd Divs, plus 201 Gds Bde and the divisional troops of one of these two divisions be amalgamated to form an infantry division for employment in ITALY.
    ….
    (d) Such divisional troops as remain unabsorbed above to become army troops, and to be disposed of to the best advantage. I should welcome any artillery, engineer, RASC or REME units or personnel that might become available in this way.

5. The proposal in para 4 (a) above would result in a division which included two Guards Brigades, and which would therefore be classified as a Guards Division. If for any reason that is considered undesirable, I

suggest that one of the Guards Brigades change places with an infantry brigade of 4 Brit Inf Div.[18]

It is interesting to note that Alexander proposed the formation of a Guards Division, likely influenced by his natural bias and experience as an officer in the Irish Guards during the First World War and Inter-War period (1911–1930). He also recognised the importance of engineers, amidst other specialist disciplines which were key to success on account of clearing the many mines and booby traps and repairing critical roads and bridges.

At that time the command of AFHQ was transitioning from General Dwight D. Eisenhower to General Henry Maitland Wilson, with the new appointment officially recorded as 16 January 1944. A memo within the Reorganisation of Formations War Diary for 17 January 1944 indicates, in a pencilled notation, that the C-in-C (Wilson), 'does not like (section) 5.B' of a report summarising Alexander's proposal of, 'Breaking up two Armd Divs and forming extra Inf Bde from Motor Bns of two Armd Bdes plus one from those employed outside formations in Mediterranean Theatre.'[19]

The CIGS sent a memo to Wilson on 19 January 1944, stating, 'whilst I am in sympathy for the need for more Infantry in ITALY I am not so happy at the idea of breaking up so many Armd Divs in view of possible requirements later on.'[20] Despite the numerous disagreements with the proposal, a number of AFHQ meetings were held through January that supported the suggestions made by Alexander. General Steele, Director of Staff Duties (DSD) at the War Office, sent a memo on 10 February acknowledging awareness of the proposals and commenting:

> Discussion has been going on actively about reorganisation of Armour …. it looks improbable that AFHQ scheme will be approved as complications on the highest level likely make it impolitic to go on with redesignation of 6 Armoured Division.[21]

While not referenced within the War Diary, it is almost certain that the War Office quashed the proposal to repurpose 6th Armoured Division to that of an infantry division. A memo from Lieutenant General Gammell, Chief of Staff AFHQ to DSD General Steele at the War Office evidences this, 'It is considered that consequent on the decision to retain 1 and 6 BRITISH Armoured Divisions, no further British Armoured Divisions are required in this theatre.'[22] The memo also raises a concern regarding the lack of availability of lorried infantry brigades in theatre.

Notwithstanding the lack of support for Alexander's suggestions, the role and structure of armoured divisions operating in Italy had to change, principally in that there would need to be a more equal balance between armour and infantry, with tanks supporting infantry rather that infantry supporting tanks.

Alexander recognised that the tactics employed by armoured divisions operating in North Africa, of tanks pushing at speed across the desert closely followed by motorised infantry were simply not possible in Italy.

CAMOUFLAGED FIST

Ken Ford eloquently sums up what happens next:

> To meet these demands, 6th Armoured Division's organisation was changed by the addition of another infantry brigade. On 21 May, 61st Infantry Brigade was formed by Brig Adrian Gore, one-time commander of 10th Rifle Brigade, and on 29 May it came under command of 6th Armoured Division. The 61st infantry Brigade was to include three battalions of the Rifle Brigade: 2nd, 7th, and 10th. The 10th Rifle Brigade was to move within the division across from 26th Armoured Brigade, retaining its organisation as a motor battalion. The other two battalions had been with Eighth Army in North Africa both as motor battalions. For the past year they had been in Egypt, where they were re-designated as 'ordinary' infantry.[23]

The discussions that led to the decision making surrounding this are not recorded in the *Reorganisation of Formations War Diary*. The first official

Printed and embroidered Rifle Brigade shoulder titles as worn by all three battalions within 61st Brigade.

mention of the formation of 61st Brigade is contained within an outgoing message from General Wilson AFHQ on 22 May 1944:

1. Under present battle conditions it has been found necessary to group Motor Bns of 7, 9 and 26 Armoured Bdes into a separate Bde to be attached to an Armoured Div. This necessitates formation of additional Bde HQ.[24]

A further outgoing message for action is recorded the next day on 26 May 1944:

1. TROOPERS have agreed to temporary formation of Bde of 3 Motor Bns but point out that they strongly deprecate use of Motor Bns in this role and difficulty of reinforcing if Bns suffer heavy casualties as no rfts can be provided from UK.

2. They therefore can only agree to formation of Bde while current ops absolutely demand it and that it must in any case be reviewed on 1 August.

3. Bde will be designated 61 Inf Bde Formation letters follow.[25]

An entry within the newly created 61st Brigade War Diary for 25 May 1944 also confirms the redesignation of 2nd and 7th Battalion Rifle Brigade:

25 [May] – 1800 – 659 Inf Tps Wksps [workshops] arrived. This completed the concentration but much remained to be done owing to 2 RB and 7 RB having to alter from Motor Bn to Inf Bn WE and Bde HQ was starting from "scratch" e.g., as regards stationery.[26]

There is some disparity between the AFHQ outgoing message and the War Diary entry of 61st Brigade in so far that AFHQ believes that all three battalions were motorised while, in fact, only 10th Battalion was.

The attachment and organisation of 61st Brigade was therefore originally intended to be for a short period of time on account of severe reinforcement challenges should it incur heavy casualties. On 8 June Alexander wrote a memo to AFHQ making the following recommendations:

1. Experience has shown conclusively that in this type of terrain an armd div requires two infantry brigades to balance the armoured component, and to maintain its momentum in enclosed country. For instance it frequently happens that the whole of an infantry brigade must be committed to drive in the enemy's outposts and to locate and pin his main line of resistance. If there is only one infantry brigade in the division a combined tank and infantry outflanking attack can only be carried out by detaching an infantry brigade from an infantry division, with consequent delay and dislocation, even in an infantry division with a brigade in reserve is within reach.

2. To provide divisions with the additional infantry brigade required to put into effect the conclusion stated in the preceding paragraph the following measure have so far been taken: -
    a) 61 Inf Bde has been formed out of the motor battalions of 7, 9 and 26 Armd Bdes and has been allocated to 6 Br Armd Div.
    b) 24 Gds Bde has been attached to 6 S.A. Armd Div.
    c) Comd 1 Cdn Corps has made urgent application to the Canadian military authorities for the allocation of another infantry brigade for 5 Cdn Arm Div.

3. After careful consideration I have come to the definite conclusion that the need for a second infantry brigade in each armoured division will continue throughout any operations that the Allied Armies in Italy may be called upon to undertake during the present war against Germany.

….

6. As regards to 61 Inf Bde I most strongly recommend for the reasons stated in para 1 above, it should be recognised as a permanent war time institution and as a regular component of 6 Br Armd Div.[27]

This was agreed on 17 June 1944 and to that end, the 61st Infantry Brigade remained with 6th Armoured Division throughout the war.

Moving from the strategic to the tactical, the composition of 1st Guards Brigade had some subtle differences compared to other infantry brigades. As a wartime service battalion the 3rd Battalion Welsh Guards differed from that of the 3rd Grenadier and 2nd Coldstream Guards Battalions in so far that it did not have colours nor did it have a Corps of Drums. Most regular foot Guards retained their drums throughout the war with the drummers doubling as stretcher-bearers. Another difference between it and those battalions serving in North-West Europe, was that carrier platoon of the support company had been converted to Vickers machine guns.[28] It is likely, that this was also the case within the other battalions of the brigade.

During 1st Guards Brigade's period of detachment from 6th Armoured Division it held key areas of the Gustav Winter Line in the Gargliano Salient, principally on the summits of Monte Ornito and Monte Cerasola in the Aurunci Mountains. Here they faced the determined German 94th Infantry Division and bitter winter conditions resulting in casualties not only from German weapons but also from frostbite and exposure. The cold was so severe that wet greatcoats froze so solidly that they would stand upright unaided. The fighting was as bitter as the weather, the ferocity of which is captured in Adam Robson's account:

> One thousand and eighty hand grenades had been thrown at the enemy, and they [2nd Battalion Coldstream Guards] had fired more mortar bombs in their 13 days there than in the whole Tunisian campaign.[29]

Map of the Monte Ornito and Cerasola area to the bottom right hand corner of Map Sheet 160-II S.E., S. Ambrogio Sul Gargliano 1:25,000.

Andrew Gibson-Watt, a replacement officer within 3rd Battalion Welsh Guards (listed in the War Diary as joining the battalion on 25 September 1944[30]), recounts in his memoirs that, 'Cerasola lived in everyone's memories as the hardest and most unpleasant experience ever.'[31]

The 2nd Battalion Coldstream Guards suffered particularly heavy losses during this period. To replenish a lost rifle company, 'S' Company of the Scots Guards[32] joined the Coldstream Guards, becoming its 4th Rifle Company on 28 March 1944 at San Potito. One week later they entered the line at Cassino.[33]

While this, again, was intended to be a short-term solution, they remained with 2nd Battalion Coldstream Guards for 12 months. Michael Curtis says:

> There were certain doubts as to whether the chemistry would be right and if this cross posting would be successful, but the Scots Guardsmen settled down very quickly in their new role.[34]

Original shoulder title worn by the Scots Guards of S Coy.

On the contrary, Andrew Gibson-Watt states:

> It was standard practice for the Foot Guards in World War Two to attach an entire company of one regiment to an understrength battalion of another. The 2nd Coldstream in our brigade had 'S' Company Scots Guards, who won high regard. In the Guards Armoured Division [who were fighting in Normandy], the doughty 'X' Coy Scots Guards fought first with the Irish Guards and then with our 1st Battalion [Welsh Guards]. The Guards were lucky to be able to do this, rather than simply draft men in and 're-badge' them as the line regiments were obliged to do.[35]

Three original variations of shoulder title worn by the men of the Coldstream Guards. There appear to have been large stocks of First World War shoulder titles held by all of the Guards regiments at the time of the Second World War. First World War examples are often seen worn in contemporary photographs. The top example with squared ends is of First World War vintage while the bottom example is very late war, perhaps 1945. All three types are seen in contemporary photographs and affixed to surviving uniform items.

Minutes from an AFHQ meeting held on 17 January 1944 (concerning the earlier outlined propositions made by Alexander) note an opinion that the Guards Brigades were better off in terms of the security of supply of replacements or reinforcements compared to ordinary Infantry regiments. With 15 months of the war left to fight at this stage, their concern for the overall resourcing situation is apparent:

> 7. PERSONNEL.
>
> Discussions then took place as to whether an additional Inf Div could be maintained from a personnel point of view. It was suggested that this would be more expensive in personnel that two Inf Bdes as integral parts of two Armd Divs.
>
> It was agreed that if we got the rfts we have asked for we could maintain our forces as constituted at present at three months intense wastage rates (the requirement being for intense rates for the months of May, June, July and August). Changing over might therefore make the personnel problem difficult,, although the problem might be eased by the fact that Gds Bdes were better off for rfts than ordinary Inf Regts.
>
> The possibility of converting Armd Regts to Div Recce Regts, in order to throw up Inf rfts which were badly needed, was then put forward but it was agreed that this would not be entirely satisfactory, particularly from the point of view of other ranks, who have little or no Inf experience, although it would ease the shortage of Inf officers.

Detail from TNA, WO 204/10206[36]

Similar to the experience of 2nd Battalion Coldstream Guards at Monte Ornito, the 3rd Battalion Welsh Guards suffered 22 killed, 90 wounded and 8 missing at Monte Piccolo during late May 1944.

	Officers		Other Ranks		Not Rank Specific	
	Killed	Wounded	Killed*	Wounded	Missing	Total
26th May 1944	0	1	2	12	0	15
27th May 1944	5	2	12	51	8	78
28th May 1944	0	2	3	19	0	24
29th May 1944	0	0	1	3	0	4
Total	5	5	18	85	8	121

*Including Died of Wounds, Detail from TNA, WO 170/1355[37]

No.2 Rifle Company was almost totally destroyed during the engagement, and the 3rd Battalion Welsh Guards War Diary records on 30 May 1944:

> STH OF MTE PICCOLO – 30 [May] – Bn re-organised on 3 Coy basis – 2 Coy L.O.B. [left out of battle]. Mobile baths throughout day. GOC and Brigadier visit Bn at 1700hrs. Draft arrives from I.R.T.D.[38]

Despite this entry, the understrength No.2 Company is often recorded within the 3rd Battalion Welsh Guards War Diary as being the reserve company during June and on until 18 July 1944. From this latter date, a company of the Grenadier Guards temporarily became the No.2 Rifle Company of the 3rd Battalion Welsh Guards:

PULICIANO – 17 [July] – C.O. went to the 'CARDIFF ARMS' to visit 2 [Gren] Coy who had just arrived. [Officers – Major WILLIS, Lieuts WHEATLEY, LEAKE and CREWDSON]. Coy appeared from all accounts to be a very good one. Most of the men were ex 6 Bn and they had come from the 201 Gds Bde. The C.O. was accompanied by the R.S.M. C.O. attended Bde Conference at 1700hrs. Mobile Bath and Cinema for Bn.

PULICIANO – 18 [July] – 2 [Gren] Coy joined the Bn and occupied billets at PULICIANO 2624.[39]

Andrew Gibson-Watt states that:

A company of Grenadiers was brought in for a few weeks to replace the lost No.2 Company…. By the time I arrived [25 September 1944] Arezzo and then Florence has been taken, the Grenadier company had departed, and the preliminary Gothic Line actions on Fifth Army's right had taken place.[40]

The 3rd Welsh Guards War Diary records that on 23 August at Ripalto, near Figline Valdarno, it received three officers and 98 other ranks from the I.R.T.D. to reinforce its numbers. In the same entry, the Diary consequently records that 2 Coy Grenadier Guard left the battalion. Gibson-Watt also recounts thereafter:

3WG had only three rifle companies, No.2 existing merely as a small cadre which did the necessary jobs such as running the battalion leave camp (Cardiff Arms) first at Lake Trasimene and then at Florence; and providing, during the winter, the corps of mule-escorts under Joe Gurney's command. Without their efforts the mule trains would not have reached their destination.[41]

'The Cardiff Arms' was the name given to Villa Pischiello, which overlooked Lake Trasimene near Passignano sul Trasimeno (see map in Chapter 5). It was used by the Welsh Guards for rest and as a L.O.B. Camp. At the time of writing (July 2023) this villa can be rented as holiday accommodation. Gibson-Watt makes reference to a second 'Cardiff Arms' in Florence, but this is unique to Gibson-Watt's account. During the winter of 1944/45 3rd Welsh Guards were positioned on the Gothic Line. The War Diary for that period continues to report officers returning to the Cardiff Arms at Trasimene, not at Florence.

During the final stages of the war 3rd Battalion Welsh Guards captured a German field cashier's truck containing the weekly pay for an entire army corps. While it is beyond doubt that this event most certainly occurred,[42] it is rumoured that men from the battalion used the seized cash to buy, amongst other things, a grand villa near Venice. It was apparently used for many years after the war by veterans and their families as a holiday destination!

Gibson-Watt also recalls that the No.2 Rifle Company was used as a 'way of resting company commanders.'[43] This was the case with his brother who was also serving within 3rd Battalion Welsh Guards, Captain (later Baron) David Gibson-Watt. David Gibson-Watt received the Military Cross three

Two original shoulder titles of the Grenadier Guards. The top title is again of First World War vintage while the lower example was manufactured during the early 1940s. Both types are seen in contemporary photographs and also affixed to surviving battledress blouses.

times before the cessation of hostilities and became a Conservative Party MP after the war.

Thus, there was a blended composition of the battalions of the 1st Guards Brigade, but nonetheless wholly composed of various regiments of the Foot Guards. As per the meeting minutes (see above) this further exemplifies the scale of the resourcing challenges met by the British Army across all theatres, but felt more acutely in Italy, predominantly due to the prioritisation of replacements to those divisions fighting in Normandy at the time.

A memo sent to the War Officer from AFHQ references these challenges on 17 March 1944:

> 3. A very large number of units have been dispatched to U.K. from this theatre during the past six months and in view of the acute BRITISH manpower shortage it is considered essential that the maximum and most economical use must be made of all BRITISH Troops in this theatre.

Detail from TNA, WO 204/10206[44]

Gibson-Watt, again, comments upon this situation, albeit much later in the campaign:

> In the last spring of the war [1945], however, the system broke down because the supply of Guardsmen simply ran out in both European theatres. In Guards Armoured Division [at that time fighting in Holland and Germany], 1WG was withdrawn and replaced by 2SG: that battalion, having absorbed 'X' Co., was

largely made up with men from other sources who had never been to Caterham. In Italy, the Light Anti-Aircraft and R.A.F. Regiment units were converted into infantry, and we were made up to strength with more than two hundred of these men. Very good fellows they were too and they loved being Guardsmen once they had discovered that life was not all drill and discipline.[45]

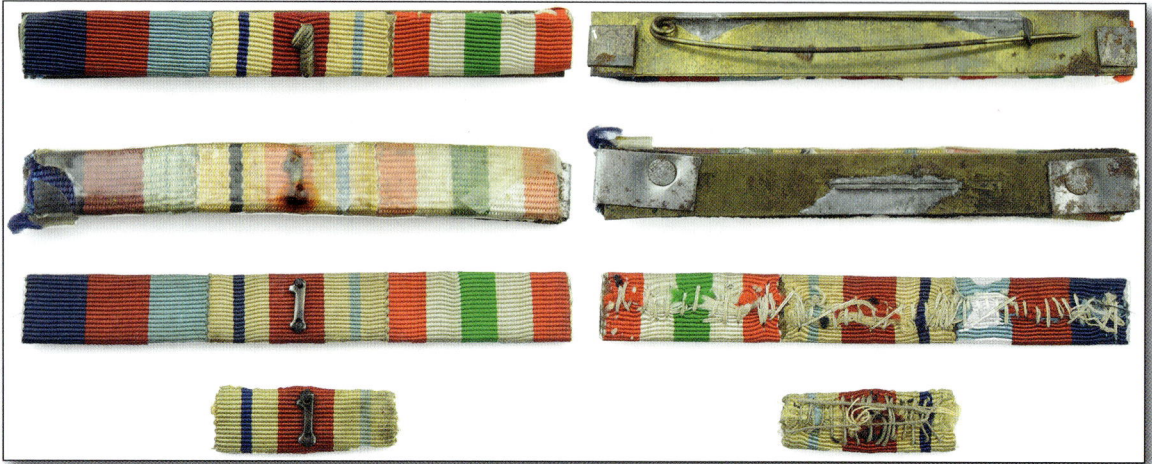

Four examples of medal ribbon bars worn by the men of 6th Armoured Division. Medals shown, left to right (triple bars): 1939–45 Star, Africa Star with 1 numeral/device denoting award of the 1st Army Bar, Italy Star. The top example is from the estate of Corporal Mathews, 3rd Battalion Welsh Guards,[46] the middle is a cellophane wrapped economy version while the bottom example is intended to be stitched to a shirt/battledress blouse. The single Africa Star ribbon bar was often worn alone, without devices, by eligible recipients in the Italian campaign. The 1st Army numeral/device became available in the second half of 1944 and is often seen worn in studio photographs taken by professional photographers near rest camps.

In summarising 6th Armoured Division, Gibson-Watt states:

The 6th Armoured was in reality regarded as Alexander's ultimate corps-de-chasse. When the final break came in the Po plain, they would thunder through as they and 7th [Armoured Division – The 'Desert Rats'] had done in Tunis, and finish the business. In the end this happened, although the rupture was in fact so general that the rest of the armies moved almost as fast.[47]

6TH ARMOURED DIVISION: INFANTRY BRIGADE COMPOSITION

Seven examples of original Welsh Guards shoulder titles. The extremely rare top example is discussed in more detail in Chapter 4. Note the differences to the obverse of each example along with the subtle variations in height, width and serif of the fonts used. It is likely that a number of the examples presented are of First World War stock kept in store until their issue and use during the Second World War. The first, second, fifth and sixth from top have direct provenance and were received from Welsh Guard veterans or their estates.

Order of Battle: 6th Armoured Division, June 1944.

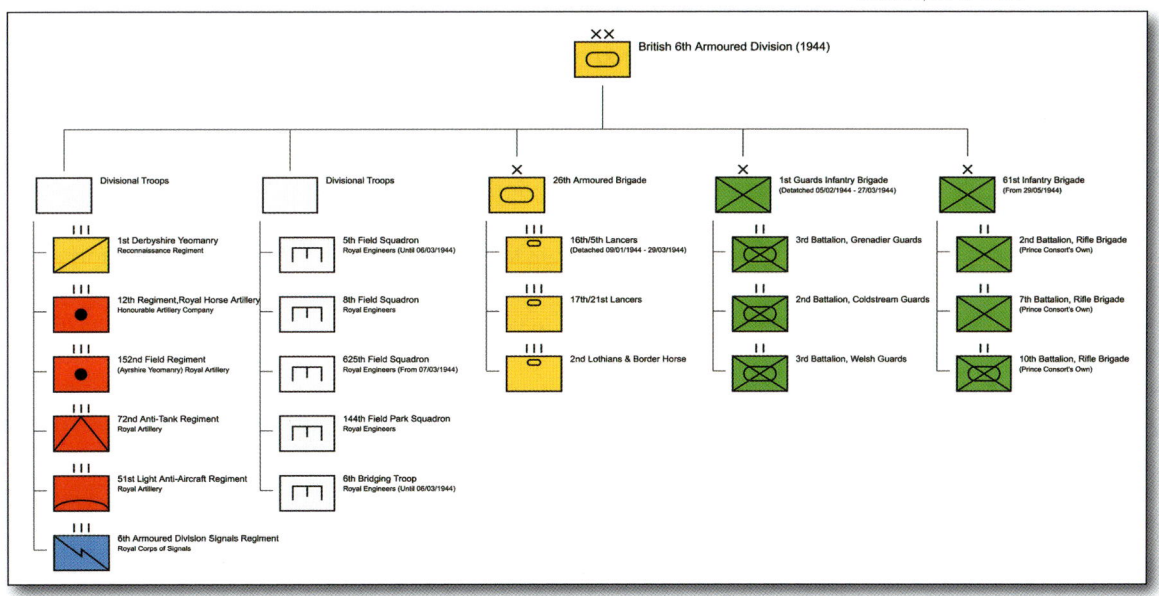

CAMOUFLAGED FIST

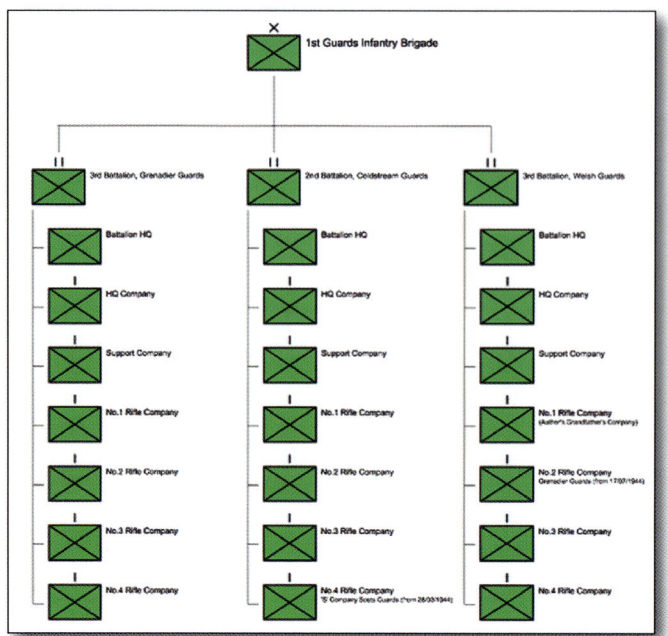

Order of Battle: 1st Guards Brigade, August 1944.[48]

A map produced immediately following the cessation of hostilities in May 1945 showing the general route taken by the bulk of 6th Armoured Division as they fought northwards through the Italian Peninsula.[49]

Chapter 3

Uniform and the Advent of the Camouflage Smocks

In contrast to the North-West European theatre, the extremes of climate in Italy led to the men of the 6th Armoured Division wearing an incredibly diverse variation of uniform items.

By early 1944, the Italian front was very much seen by the Allies to be of secondary importance, effectively a sideshow to the impending offensive in Northern France. In preparation for this, it was necessary to stockpile equipment and uniform for 21st Army Group for the coming invasion. Consequently, the forces on the 'second front' were increasingly equipped, from 1943 on, with items made within theatre, the U.S. (via War Aid), along with those made throughout the British Empire. This is seen in the continued and prolific use of Short Magazine Lee Enfield's No.1 Mk IIIs (herein referred to as SMLE) rather than the newer No.4 Mk1 (herein referred to as No.4) and U.S. made Thompson submachine guns (herein referred to as Thompson) in lieu of the Sten submachine gun.

The ubiquitous British woollen battledress was arguably the most modern combat uniform of its time and had been specifically designed with the needs of mechanised infantry in mind. It was both hard wearing and warm, even when wet. It was the principal uniform used by British and Commonwealth Forces throughout the war. The arrival of U.S. made War Aid battledress in theatre was well received as it was of a finer wool and thus more comfortable than the British or its Commonwealth counterparts. This was greener in colour and a hybrid of the earlier serge battledress and that of the austerity pattern. Indian made Aertex (a soft and open-weave fabric which gave both good ventilation and protection from the sun) battledress was also used throughout the campaign although the author is unable to locate any photographic evidence of their use within 6th Armoured Division specifically.

Denim battledress overalls produced initially from brown, and then khaki green, cotton were also used extensively. These were intended to be worn over the battledress as work-wear and as a result were issued in a size larger than woollen battledress. It was lighter than the woollen counterparts and inevitably looser, cooler and more comfortable in the heat. As such, it was used extensively in lieu of the wool battledress throughout the campaign. Gas capes were also frequently used for protection from the rain.

In an Empire that stretched around the globe the British Army had a long history of fighting in hot climates. This led to the introduction, in tropical climates, of a lightweight, dust-coloured uniform which both provided some camouflage and was reasonably practical and comfortable. This khaki uniform (named from the Urdu word *khak* for dust) had been in use since the late nineteenth century and was referred to as khaki drill (often abbreviated to KD). The majority of Allied forces fighting in Italy in 1944 had fought in North Africa and consequently had large stocks of, and a great fondness for, khaki drill wear. Numerous khaki drill items were used including a variety of shorts, shirts, bush jackets and trousers. They were ideal for the warmer months in Southern Italy. Khaki drill trousers were also prized for their bartering power as Bowlby recounts at Cantaloupe in June 1944:

> When the Platoon had checked their equipment the section commanders came round making lists of deficiencies. Officially this only covered anything lost or damaged in action. In fact it gave us an opportunity to get something for nothing and we made the most of it. Half of the Platoon put in for emergency rations and khaki drill trousers. We had discovered that trousers fetched a higher price from the farmers than anything else. The number of pairs listed as 'Lost in Battle' must have run into the tens of thousands.[50]

By mid–1944, more durable U.S. made herringbone twill bush shirts and jackets also appeared in theatre. U.S. mustard coloured enlisted man woollen shirts were also issued extensively to British forces. By December, specific winter clothing was issued to those facing the *Grüne Linie* (more commonly referred to as the Gothic Line) in the Northern Apennines. These included white snow oversuits, anoraks and short white duffle coats augmenting the issue greatcoats.

The standard Pattern 37 web equipment was used by all British and Commonwealth troops and it can be seen in photographs worn with and without blanco.

What was worn, carried and displayed on uniforms was dictated at battalion level with the War Diaries frequently stipulating detailed dress instructions within daily orders. Italy was not declared malaria free until the 1950s and consequently Anti-Malarial Precaution orders were contained within the War Diaries. This inevitably contributed to decision making surrounding dress:

```
(iv)  Anti-Malarial Precautions.
      (a) One week's supply of Mepacrine will be taken.
      (b) Each man will take his bottle of Mosquito Repellant.
          NOTE: It is vitally important that paras (a) and (b)
                above are strictly complied with. The CO will
                hold offrs personally responsible for seeing this is
                done.
      (c) Flit guns, Flysol, Malarial will be taken by pls. Those for
          convenience should be carried in empty bottles.
      (d) Anti-mosquito veils when in possession will be taken and used
          by sentries at the discretion of Coy Comds.
```

Detail from TNA, WO 170/1355[51]

UNIFORM AND THE ADVENT OF THE CAMOUFLAGE SMOCKS

This may have contributed to an order issued on 3 May 1944 by the 3rd Battalion Grenadier Guards on 3 May 1944 at Cassino:[52]

> 3. KHAKI DRILL.
> Khaki Drill will not be worn until ordered.

Likewise, a further entry on 9 May 1944 states:[53]

> 3. ANTI-MALARIAL PRECAUTIONS ETC.
> All ranks are again reminded that trousers must be worn and shirt sleeves rolled down after sundown (at present 1930 hrs). To guard against chills, cardigans or battle-dress blouses will also be worn after sun-down.

April 1944, 3rd Battalion Welsh Guards at Cassino:[54]

> ADM.
> 10. Dress. Jerkin order. large pack containing two blankets. and Small kit. Gas cape rolled. 2 sandbags att to person.
> 11. Food. 48 hrs dry rations in sandbag. Fighting ration to be carried. Emergency Ration in pocket.
> 12. Cooking. Tommy Cookers.
> 13. Water. Drinking water will be brought up. It will be doubly disinfected. Washing - in shell holes. Well at Tac H.Q.
> Sheet 2/......

The same order also makes reference to the wearing of gym shoes (plimsolls) or sandbags over boots to enable silent movement while patrolling.

> 18. Pests. Rats - poison.
> Bodies - De-odoriants.
> 19. Silent movement. Patrol boots - sandbags - gym shoes.

14 April 1944, 3rd Battalion Welsh Guards at Cassino.[55]

> 2. DRESS.
> Jerkin Order - large pack containing one blanket and small kit - one blanket round pack - gascape rolled. 2 sandbags att to person plus 2 sandbags carried to be put on feet at 'A' Ech for silent movement. Cap comforter - no berets to be taken. 50 rds or equivalent to be carried.

CAMOUFLAGED FIST

Men of the 3rd Battalion Welsh Guards at San Angelo Church, Cassino on 19 May 1944. Note the wearing of battledress complete with formation signs and shoulder titles (albeit obliterated by the censor). Also see the gym shoes (plimsolls) worn by the guardsmen top and bottom right (with German MG42 Machine Gun), and the guardsman centre left pulling a sandbag over his ammo boots. It is likely that they are about to commence a patrol to round up surrendering German troops.[56] (Photograph courtesy of Neil Powell, www.battlefieldhistorian.com)

The 3rd Battalion Grenadier Guards Diary also gave specific instructions regarding the divisional formation signs while khaki drill was worn:[57]

```
4. KHAKI DRILL.
    1. When K.D. is taken into use the Division signs will continue to be worn.
    2. Officers and W.Os. will wear them on the sleeves attached either by press
       studs or sewing.
    3. N.C.Os. and Guardsmen will wear them on the shoulder epaulette, by sewing
       the sign on to a band which can be slipped over the epaulette thus allowing
       easy removal before washing.
       All N.C.Os. and Guardsmen at present in possession of Div signs will have
       them prepared for wearing with K.D. forthwith.
    4. Instructions as to the wearing of designations with K.D. will be issued
       later.
```

The author's collection contains examples of both Officer/W.O. and NCO/guardsman Mailed Fist formation signs conforming to the orders stipulated in Sections 2 and 3 of the diary entry.

The Mailed Fist formation badge below conforms to the regulation for wear by officers and warrant officers. The badge features four press studs to the rear fastened with khaki cotton thread. The badge has also been reinforced with a piece of celluloid (similar to that used in map cases) that has been cut to size and affixed using a thicker white cotton thread. The badge face has been painted black around the fist itself to disguise the white and khaki thread used.

Similarly, the use of press studs for attachment of shoulder titles can be seen on the illustration. This embroidered Welsh Guards title is of the rarest

UNIFORM AND THE ADVENT OF THE CAMOUFLAGE SMOCKS

This photograph shows an original field made pair of epaulette sliders. They have been fashioned from, what appears to be, an Aertex khaki drill belt. This has been fastened to make a band with black cotton thread and pins. The formation signs have then been stitched to the band in the same black cotton thread. Note that the formation badges are not an identical matching pair, a number of 1st Guards Brigade groupings owned by the author often include mismatched formation signs but with identical wear and attachment thread evidencing that they were worn together.

wartime type. The reverse of the title has been sewn with black cotton thread to a matching shaped piece of khaki drill material to which three press studs were attached. This would then correspond with three fasteners stitched to the shirt or battledress blouse. While the press studs have long since been lost, clear evidence of their presence remain.

Given the frequent short distance changes in environment and landscape encountered, and despite the highly regulated dress orders, there are numerous

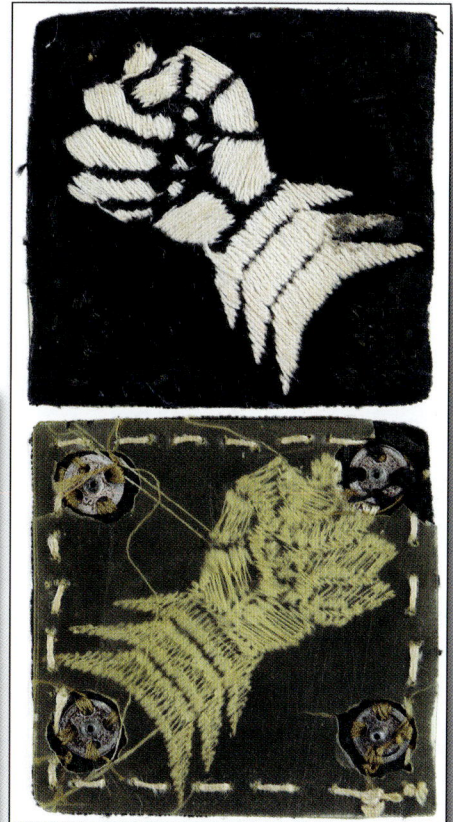

CAMOUFLAGED FIST

photographs of various mixtures of wool and denim battledress with khaki drill items worn together often with the issue woollen pullover (officially 'the Cardigan'). Khaki drill, while excellent camouflage in the desert of North Africa and Southern Italy would not be suitable for the green and lush grass landscape of Umbria and Tuscany in the height of summer. Both wool and denim battledress would also have been too warm. A new environment and a new problem was ahead.

With the exception of the face veil and blanco, personal camouflage largely comprised of that contained within a 1944 training pamphlet, *Fieldcraft, Battle Drill, Section and Platoon Tactics*.[58]

This future need had already been identified sometime before May 1944 and mitigated through the production of a loose, and therefore cool, sleeveless one-size-fits-all smock made from Italian M1929 *Telo Mimetico* camouflaged material that could be worn over a shirt or battledress blouse. This garment presented a perfect tactical solution to both the hot climate and the environment encountered, being easily carried, light to wear and enabled the wearer to more effectively blend in with his surroundings. It perfectly illustrates the innovation and adaptations made to meet the demands of this most arduous of theatres.

The need for this smock was such that even the Guards of 1st Guards Brigade, with their strict standards of uniform and etiquette, embraced this unofficial garment. As a vanguard regular army unit, they had already faced

Fieldcraft, Battle Drill, Section and Platoon Tactics

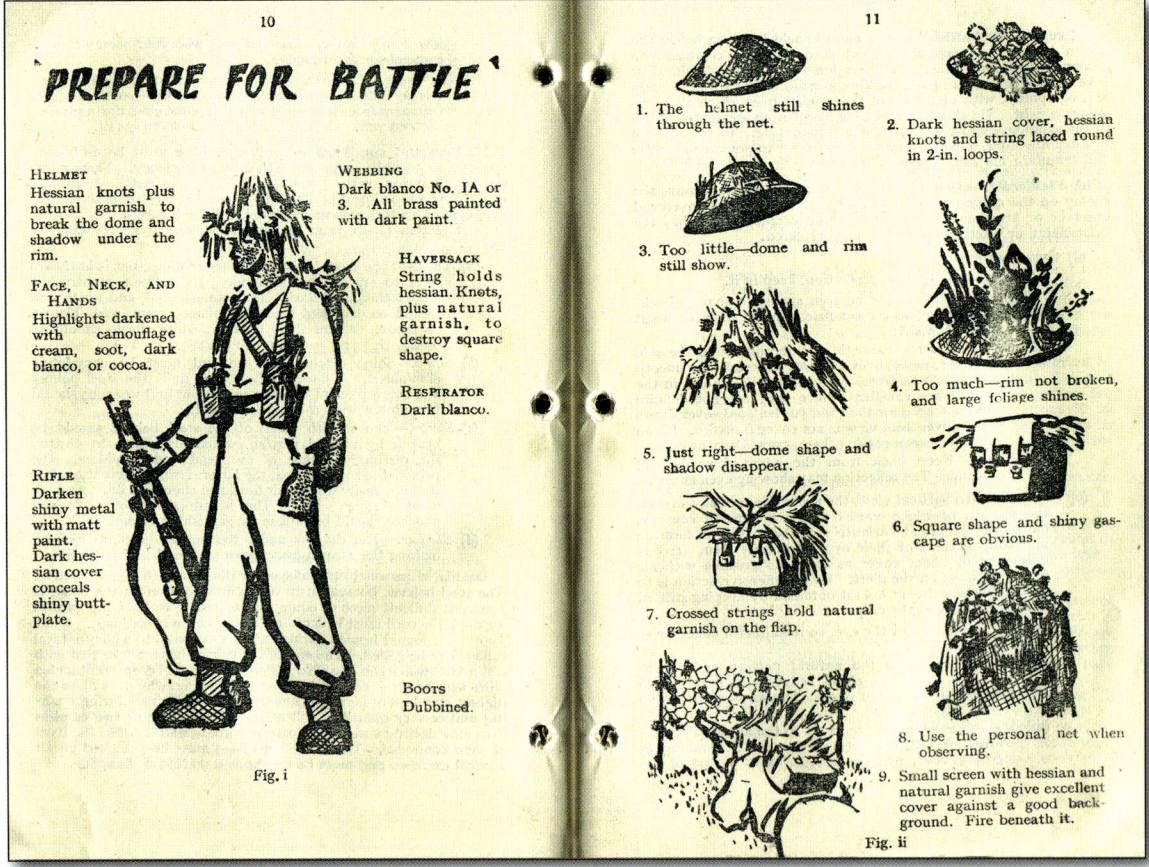

some of the most elite and proficient veteran troops that Germany had in Italy; it is highly likely they would have welcomed any change that provided even the slightest advantage to give them an edge and increase their survivability. A later chapter setting out use of this garment will provide further insight regarding its use from those who wore them.

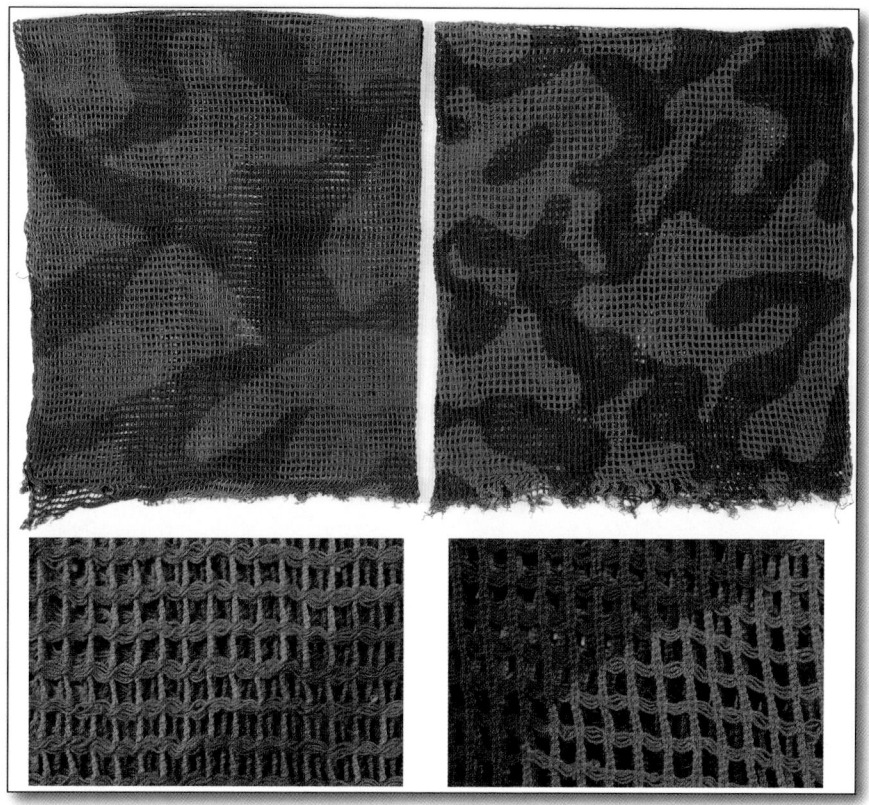

Issued from 1942, the face veil was a green and brown camouflage scrim net used to aid personal concealment. Its principle purpose was to be draped over a man's back and shoulders to break up any outline of his shape and/or equipment. They could be used over the head permitting the solder to see without his own face being seen, or erected as a net screen to conceal a firing position. They were very popular and are most often seen in photographs used as a scarf. Two variations are presented here, complete with detail of the weave construction: an early war pattern (left) measuring 102cm × 71cm and late war 'ghost' pattern (right) measuring 99cm × 79cm.[59]

Contrary to popular belief, blancoed webbing was used extensively in Italy. A photograph in the author's collection of the NCOs from No.1 Rifle Company, 3rd Welsh Guards, (the author's great grandfather, Glyn Spowart, is in the back row, fourth from left) illustrates the use of blancoed and unblancoed/scrubbed/sun-bleached webbing simultaneously. Also note the different colours and styles of wear of cap comforters in addition to the sporadic use of Welsh Guards shoulder titles (Colour Plate D recreates an NCO from this image.) While the photograph is marked on the back with 'August 1944', it matches a number of other photographs taken on 11 July 1944 in the Bone area, Cortona prior to the assault on Monte Lignano.[60]

CAMOUFLAGED FIST

This has on the reverse 'August 1944. With the compliments of MAJOR R. C. SHARPLES M.C. 3rd Battln (sic). WELSH GUARDS C.M.F.' Major Sharples M.C. commanded 1st Coy and survived the war. He was assassinated in 1973 while serving as Governor of Bermuda.

Further detail.

UNIFORM AND THE ADVENT OF THE CAMOUFLAGE SMOCKS

The Riccardo Bizzaro collection contains a large pack and haversack owned by a member of 2nd Battalion Coldstream Guards and a large pack stamped to a guardsman of 3rd Battalion Grenadier Guards. They were found together during a house clearance in Monselice near Padua, Italy. Both battalions were present in the area for a short time before the end of the war.

(Photograph courtesy of Riccardo Bizzaro)

The Coldstream Guards haversack (left) has been initially blancoed with Khaki Green Light 103 (KG103) and then over-blancoed with Khaki Green 3 (KG3). The accompanying large pack (centre) only being blancoed in KG3. The large pack from the 3rd Battalion Grenadier Guards (right) has been blancoed in KG103 only. The KG103 colouring was used from 1940 with KG3 being seen later in the war from spring 1944 onwards.

No reference whatsoever to approved blanco colourings can be found within any of the War Diaries of the six battalions of 6th Armoured Division. It is likely that webbing was blancoed, scrubbed and then re-blancoed depending on the situation, environment and terrain being encountered to provide additional camouflage as per the stipulations of the infantry training pamphlet discussed earlier in this chapter.

Bowlby recounts the appearance of a deceased guardsman at Cantalupo evidencing the use of blanco by the Guards on 10–11 June 1944:

> a leg stuck out from under a blanket. Everything about it was just so: the trouser had a knife-edge crease, the gaiter was freshly blancoed, the boot polished. You could see it mounting guard all by itself.[61]

See Chapter 8 and Appendices I, II and III for contemporary and modern photographs illustrating the variety of uniforms worn by the infantryman of 6th Armoured Division.

Chapter 4

M1929 *Telo Mimetico* Camouflage

Many nations experimented with camouflage clothing during the First World War although the Italian Army were the first to adopt a mass-produced printed pattern in 1929, the *M1929 Telo Mimetico* pattern (1929 Model Camouflage Cloth). Such was the effectiveness of this pattern that, in somewhat modernised form, it continued as the principal camouflage pattern of the Italian Army into the 1990s.

The print comprises of a generally wavy pattern of greyish-green, tan/ochre and chocolate brown complete with sharply printed twig like off-shoots. It was printed on one side only, the reverse being undyed. There were five colour variations manufactured over the 14 or so years of pre-war and wartime production. The pattern was scaled down somewhat before the outbreak of World War Two, and this resulted in some lengthwise compression of the original pattern and was likely implemented to reduce roll size and thus facilitate smaller scale production. Generally, later patterns become brighter with the print becoming less defined and crisp.[62]

The most extensive use of the pattern by the Italian Army was as a 185cm square multipurpose rain poncho/shelter section/groundsheet named the *Telo Tenda*, literally translating as 'tent cloth'. This item was used in a similar fashion to the better known German *Zeltbahn 31*, which itself was printed in the German *Splittertarn* pattern but was triangular rather than square. Later in the war some *Telo Mimetico* material was also produced in the *Zeltbahn 31* triangular shape and issued to German troops.

In order to use it as a poncho, the *Telo Tenda* had a central shaped opening to allow the head to be inserted through the fabric, which was then secured by buttons. The four corners were then buttoned back to the underside (to make an octagonal shape) as seen on the illustrations below. The *Telo Tenda* was also supplied with accessories including pegs, a pole and guy lines to enable it to become a shelter.[63] It could also be fastened to other *Telo Tenda* to make more complex tent structures. (See Appendix IV for further narrative, images and diagrams from the instruction pamphlet.)

M1929 *TELO MIMETICO* CAMOUFLAGE

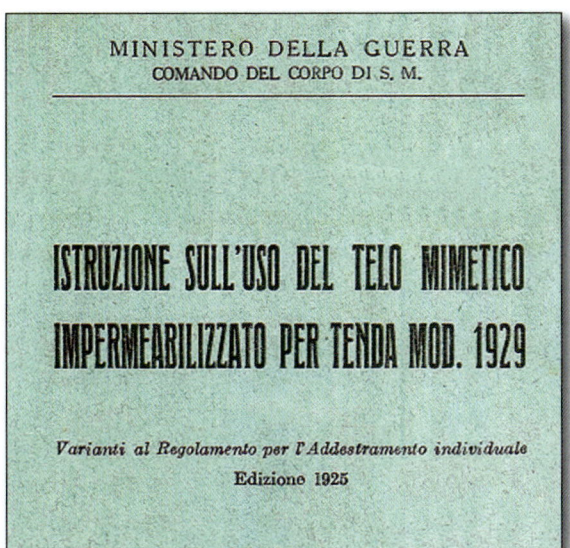

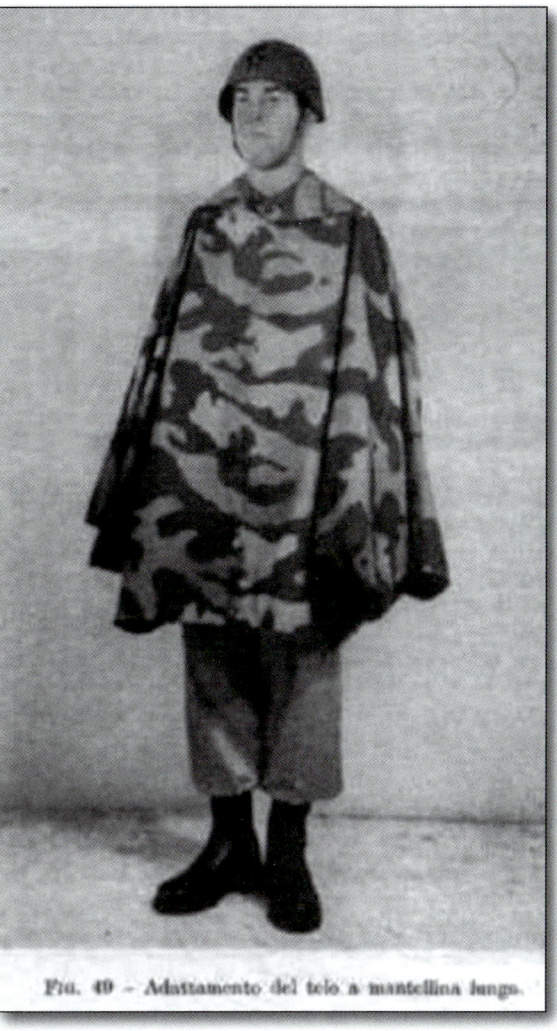

Fig. 40 - Adattamento del telo a mantellina lunga.

The pattern was used to produce some specialist garments for paratroopers and other specialised troops, most notably a smock for the elite *Divisione Folgore* (185th Paratroop Division of the Italian Army) in 1942.

After the Italian surrender in 1943 large quantities of the pattern were seized by the Germans and repurposed to make a variety of bespoke garments including caps, tunics, trousers and fur lined winter coats amongst other items. There is some debate amongst historians and collectors as to whether the Germans commenced *official* factory fabrication of issue garments in the pattern or not. What is certain is that the 1st and 12th *Waffen-SS* Panzer Divisions (*Leibstandarte* and *Hitlerjugend* respectively) made extensive use of the pattern alongside a mix of standard issue *Waffen-SS* uniforms and equipment. This is evidenced in numerous photographs taken during the Normandy Campaign in June, July and August 1944. Inevitably stocks were seized by the Allies also, most notably in Naples in early 1944. The camouflage smocks used by 6th Armoured Division were made by repurposing these captured Italian *Telo Tenda*.

CAMOUFLAGED FIST

Above: Officers of 12th SS Panzer Division *Hitlerjugend*, taken early June 1644 at Abbaye D'Ardenne, Caen. Left to right, *Obersturmbannführer* Heinz Milius, C.O. III/25 SS PzGR Rgt in discussion with Divisional Operations Officer *Sturmbannführer* Hubert Meyer, individual unidentified, *Obersturmführer* Bernhard Meitzel.[64]

Right: A colourised version of an original photograph taken on 9 June 1944 at Rots, Normandy. Left to right: *Unterscharführer* Peter Koslowski (*Adjutant III Zug*), individual unidentified, *Obersturmbannführer* Max Wünsche (*C.O. SS Panzer Regiment 12, Hitlerjugend*) wounded with bandaged head and Italian Camouflage, Oberschütze Klaus Schuh (*soldat in 3 Gruppe / III Zug*), *Sturmmann* Otto Funk (in the background, *soldat in 3 Gruppe / III Zug*), *Hauptscharführer* Wilhelm Boigk (*Zugführer III Zug*), and *Hauptsturmführer* Rudolf von Ribbentrop (*Chef 3 Kompanie / I Abteilung / SS Panzer Regiment 12 Hitlerjugend* and son of Joachim von Ribbentrop, Third Reich Minister for Foreign affairs).[65]

M1929 *TELO MIMETICO* CAMOUFLAGE

The wearing of an identical camouflage pattern to that used by the enemy does not come without risk of friendly fire. Nevertheless, this behaviour was not limited to the Italian campaign, it was also undertaken in North-West Europe as evidenced in this photograph taken at a sniper school, presumably in educating student snipers. The smock worn in this case is a Waffen-SS Oak leaf pattern print smock.[66]

CAMOUFLAGED FIST

Ron Volstad, the well-known illustrator, shared this image with the author. It shows a young soldier from the South Saskatchewan Regiment, 2nd Canadian Infantry Division at Groningen, Holland in 1945. The Telo Mimetico jacket worn is of the exact pattern as that used by the *12th Waffen-SS Panzer Division Hitlerjugend* in Normandy, which is where he most likely acquired it. The wear of non-standard uniform in the Canadian Army was prohibited which may indicate that he might have been a sniper or a scout where this ruling was generally relaxed.

Joseph De Freitos, Pont Brocard, Normandy, 28 July 1944, 41st Armoured Infantry Regiment, 2nd U.S. Armoured Division. There is anecdotal information that an experimental deployment of a two-piece herringbone twill camouflage uniform by the 2nd U.S. Armoured Division caused friendly fire incidents in Normandy. The uniform was similar to that used by the U.S. Marine Corps in the Pacific Theatre and is cited to have been often mistaken for Waffen-SS camouflage pattern clothing. Their use exists in the photographic record for the U.S. 2nd Armoured Division between June and September 1944, but there is no firm evidence to suggest that friendly fire events actually happened, and one would have expected frequent instances to result in the prompt withdrawal of the trial. (Photograph courtesy of Neil Powell, www.battlefieldhistorian.com)

Chapter 5

Evidence, Photographs and Chronology

Personal accounts, documentation and the photographic record all suggest a timeline of use of the camouflaged smocks from May to December 1944. There is no mention or photographic record of their use after the winter of 1944.

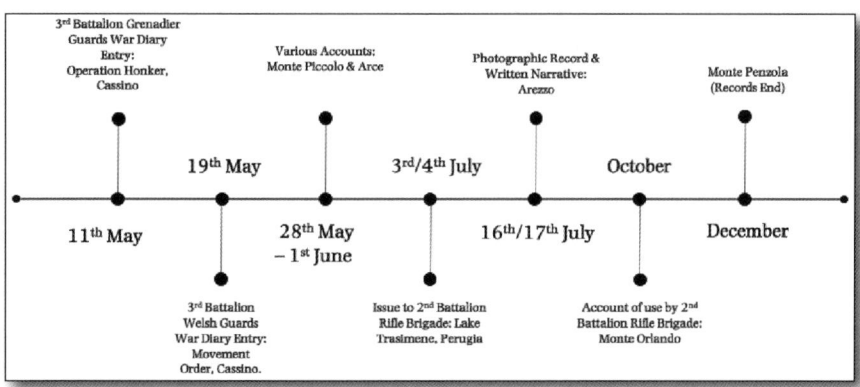

A timeline of use of the smocks.

The earliest official reference to the garment is detailed within an 'Admin Instruction' dated 11 May 1944 contained within an Appendix of the 3rd Grenadier Guards War Diary relating to Operation Honker. Operation Honker constituted the British element of the wider Operation Diadem which led to the breaching of the Gustav Line via the fall of Cassino, and enabled the breakout into the Liri Valley and opened the road to Rome. 1st Guards Brigade's role for Operation Honker was fourfold:

1. to firmly hold their existing positions within Cassino town to prevent any German spoiling attack
2. to simulate an attack in the town itself
3. to closely observe any signs of withdrawal by the enemy
4. to assist in the rounding up of the German garrison

CAMOUFLAGED FIST

Excerpt of Map Sheet 160 (1:100,000) Cassino (GSGS 4164 series) reproduced by 514 Survey Company, Royal Engineers. April 1944. This section illustrates the operational area for 6th Armoured Division during May 1944.

EVIDENCE, PHOTOGRAPHS AND CHRONOLOGY

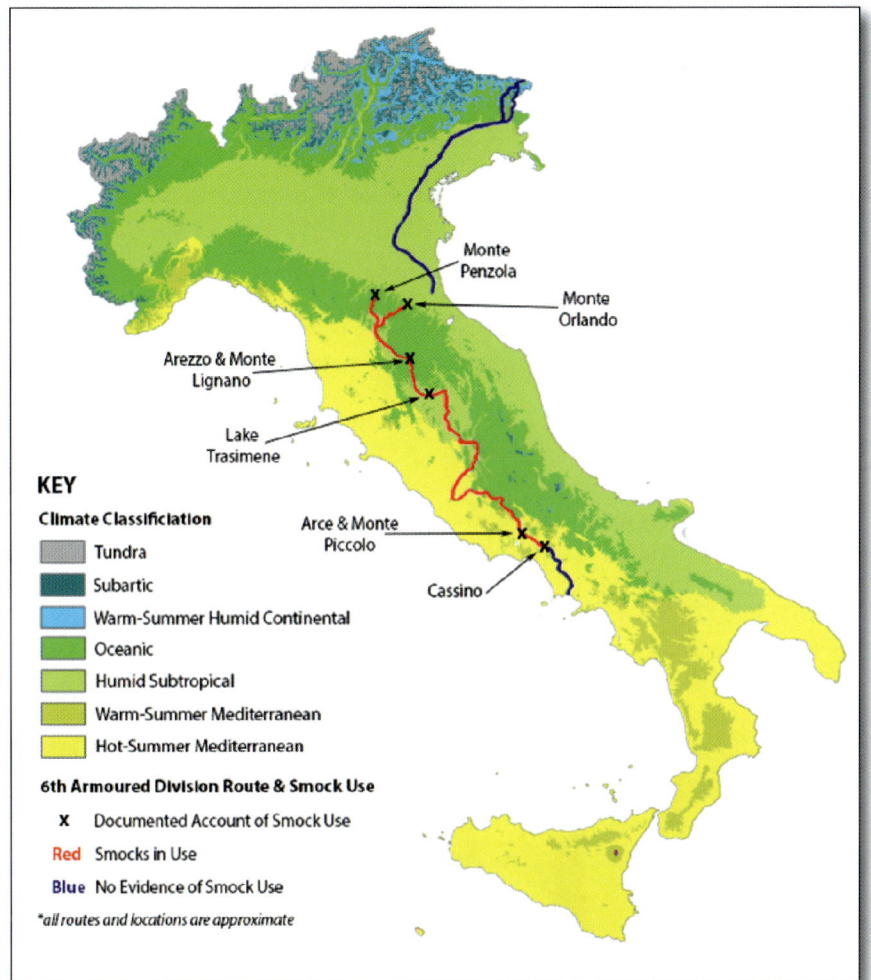

Juxtaposition of the route taken by the 6th Armoured Division through Italy denoting confirmed areas where the smocks were used overlaid against a Köppen Climate Classification Chart. This demonstrates the changing environment and climates being faced and shows the need for the use and deployment of the smocks.

The Admin Section of the document gives the following order:

BD will be taken to ensure everyone has one suit with him. Best suits will remain 'B' Ech. Smocks will be taken in bulk by Q.M. Denim trousers will be issued to all ranks in 'F' Ech later.[67]

```
6.    ADMIN
      (i)   Petrol Tins
            All four gall petrol tins at present held by Coys will be handed in to
            MTO by 1800 hrs 11 May.
      (ii)  Water Cans
            QM will issue available 2 gall water cans in concentration area.
      (iii) Latrine Seats
            The Pioneer Offr will arrange for one 3 seater to be available for
            each Coy to take fwd.
      (iv)  Tentage
            Normal ten-man battle tentage will be taken.  QM will arrange for 400
            bivvies to be taken to concentration area 12 May.
      (v)   Blankets
            One blanket per man is to be handed in, in the near future.
            One blanket will remain at "B" Ech.  One blanket only will be with
            man in concentration area.
      (vi)  Greatcoats
            Those greatcoats not at present with Bn will be taken fwd.
```

63

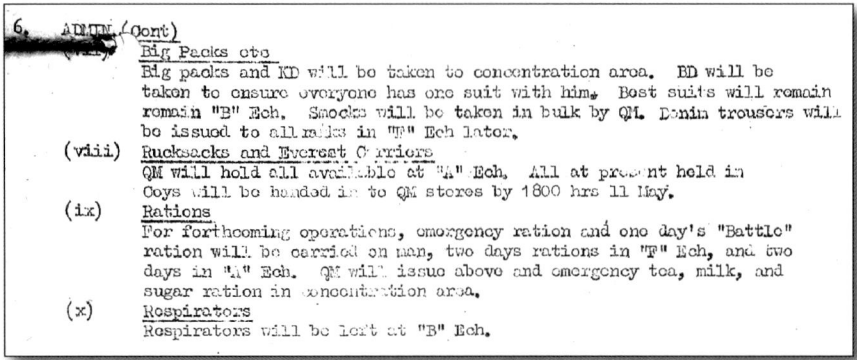

As discussed in Chapter 3 (and shown in the photographs in Appendix II), it is known that battledress was being worn by 1st Guards Brigade in Cassino town. What is interesting is that this Admin Instruction demonstrates the prior recognition that alternative clothing will be required for the subsequent breakout operations likely in acknowledgement of the forthcoming anticipated change in environment.

The phrase 'smocks will be taken in bulk' may suggest that they had not yet been issued to the Grenadier Guards *per se*. It also implies that they were naturally already available to the battalion, and therefore likely the rest of the brigade, in early May 1944.

A similar instruction is found within the 3rd Battalion Welsh Guards War Diary in respect of Operation Honker on 9 May 1944, also acknowledging that khaki drill wear may soon be required as well:[68]

```
6.  K.D.
        Orders re K.D. will be issued separately.
```

There is no documented evidence of the use of the garments by 6th Armoured Division within Cassino itself, and this is wholly logical. There would be limited need for the use of camouflage smocks given the subterranean troglodyte existence endured by the Guards, the patrolling by night only and the description of the terrain given by guardsmen on 18 May (see the photograph in Appendix I), where:

> For the first time, the men were able to come out into the sun, and gaze around them at the scene of devastation they had lived in so long without being able to see more than a small part. Cassino did indeed look very different in day-light .... the shattered buildings stone merged with powdered rock [which] .... glistened white in the sun. Even the bare earth was covered by a thick layer of white dust, broken by great cauldrons of black water where a bomb had fallen.[69]

There is photographic evidence of the use of the smocks during Operation Diadem by the Polish Corps, but their area of operations was beyond the destroyed town itself.

EVIDENCE, PHOTOGRAPHS AND CHRONOLOGY

An entry in the 3rd Battalion Welsh Guards War Diary dated 19 May 1944 contains a Warning Order relating to their movement to a peace harbour at San Pietro, east of Cassino (the site of a bloody battle fought by the Americans), in readiness for the advance up the Liri Valley. Under the subtitle of 'Admin' it states:

> <u>Dress</u>. Q.M. to arrange for distribution of denim trousers, Camouflage smocks. Rifle Coys to complete their quota of 110 per Coy. Q.M. to arrange for distribution of required number of denim blouses to Sp Coy from Rifle Coys to complete their requirements.[70]

This document is important as it sets out the number of garments issued to each Company (110). The reference made to the distribution of denim trousers is also noteworthy and matches the instruction outlined in the 3rd Grenadier Guards War Diary, their wear being evidenced in a number of photographs two months later in mid-July. From this it can be established that at least 440 camouflage smocks were issued to 3rd Welsh Guards and likely more, given other accounts of use by field officers discussed later.

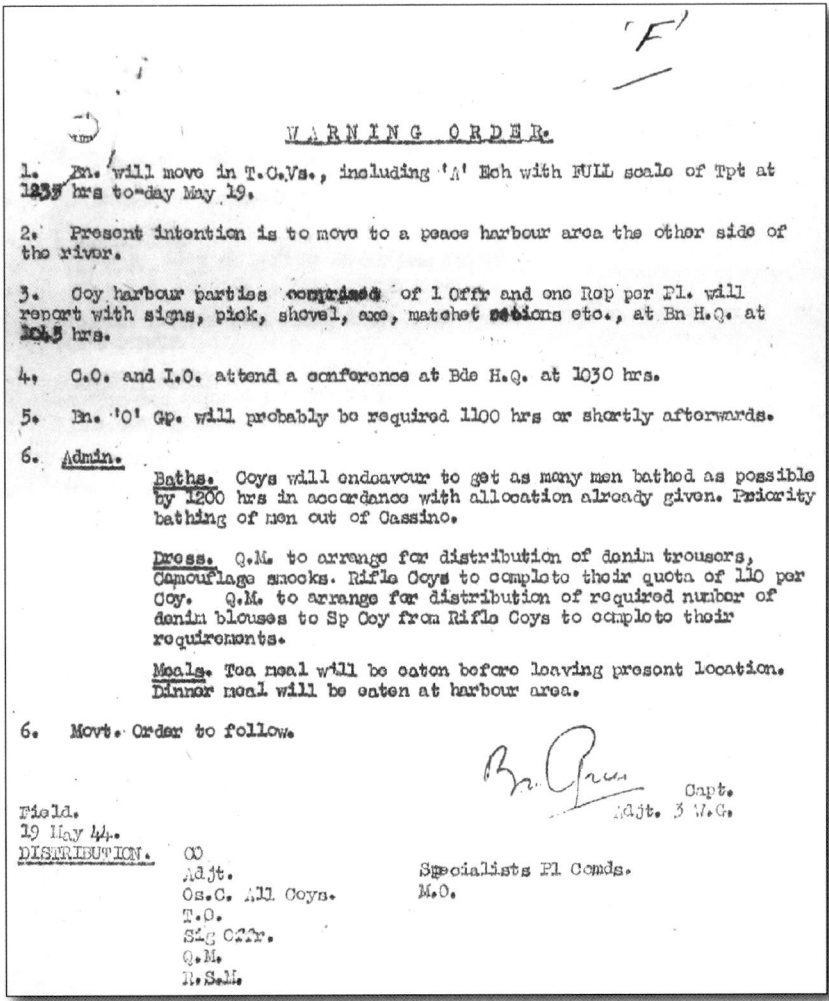

The first photograph of the infantrymen of 6th Armoured Division wearing camouflaged smocks was taken of the men of 3rd Battalion Grenadier Guards on 26 May, just after they had crossed the River Melfa and heading towards Arce Note the face veil used as a camouflaged helmet cover by the guardsman in the left foreground.

(Photograph courtesy of Neill Powell, www.battlefieldhistorian.com)

This advance would result in 1st Guards Brigade soon becoming engaged in the bloody battles to secure Monte Piccolo, Grande and Orio, which dominated the Route 6 pass between Coldragone and Arc, between 26 and 29 May.

The 1st Guards Brigade War Diary records:

26 [May] – ... At 1100hrs 3 Gren Gds, mounted on the tanks of 16/5 L [Lancers], move fwd and cross the river by the ford at 699259. The crossing is made without oppseitions (*sic*), and the adv is rapid. By 1500 hrs 3 Gren Gds, now adv through very close country on foot, with the tks in close sp. Report the line COLDRAGONE-CESE clear. They consolidate on this line for about an hr, and then push fwd behind the tks of 16/5 L, towards the pass at 669. On approaching the high ground on either side of the pass a few enemy M.G's open up and Route 6 which is the main axis of adv is heavily mortared and shelled. 3 Gren Gds lose about 20 casualties and it is decided to form a firm base on COLDRAGONE –

CESE while the armour probd (*sic*) fwd. During the afternoon 3 WG, mounted on the tks of 2 L & B H [Lothian & Border Horse] move across the River MELFA and conc at 709255.[71] The armour makes little headway in the very close country short of ARCE, and it becomes evident during the afternoon that the town will not fall today.[72]

Following the battle for Monte Piccolo, Grande and Orio, and nine days after the original Warning Order citing the distribution of camouflage smocks, the below photograph was taken by Sgt Johnson and officially captioned as:

EIGHTH ARMY. THE BATTLE FOR ARCE NA15688. A Sherman tank passes Arce signpost. 3rd Welsh Guards, Arce. Taken by Sgt. Johnson 28.5.44. Tank: 2 Lothians, Border Horse (26 A/Bde, 6th A/Div). (Image, open source. Caption Imperial War Museum, NA15668.)

The same photograph is annotated by Philip Brutton in his account:[73]

The Sherman tanks of the 2nd Lothian and Border Horse which were to take us out of the battle [Monte Piccolo and Monte Orio], 8 Platoon, 3 Company, 3rd Bn Welsh Guards

Philip Brutton is pictured second from left sitting on the rear deck of the Sherman. While not easily discernible to the untrained eye, the Guardsmen are wearing camouflaged smocks. Also note the Bren gun and 'biscuit tin cookers' strapped to the rear of the Sherman.

Mistakes are often made in annotations by war photographers and it is believed that this photograph was taken on 29 May 1944 rather than 28 May as it is labelled, that is the day following the German withdrawal. 1st Guards Brigade War Diary gives credence to this:

> 29 [May] – At Dawn the Lothian Force, with coy 3 WG under comd, advanced up Route Six towards ARCE, which was entered at 0845 hrs by the leading tks. On the capture of the town bns were withdrawn off M. PICCOLO to harbour areas just South of the feature, where they were put on 3 hrs notice to move. The coy 3 WG was withdrawn from u/c 2 Lothians at 1500hrs. Bns spent the day in rest and in burying their dead. 10 prisoners were collected from the slopes of M. GRANDE and M. PICCOLO, who had remained behind in an exhausted or wounded condition, and over 90 German dead were counted on the southern slopes of M. PICCOLO alone. 6 Brit Armd Div has been promised a few days rest, handing over the pursuit of the enemy to 8 Ind Div.
>
> 30 [May] – Bde HQ moves to 660278. Bns remain in the same positions.[74]

Given the earlier Warning Order issued on 19 May 1944, and their use by the Grenadier Guards en-route to Arce and the evidence within this photograph, it is beyond doubt that the smocks were worn by both the Welsh and Grenadier Guards during the battles for the hills near Coldragone.

A simultaneous account given by Michael Curtis,[75] in his book covering the exploits of S Coy Scots Guards, says that immediately following the battle of Monte Piccolo (likely 1 June 1944):

(S Coy) had time to reorganise and take care of casualties, and at the same time, arrange for a change in dress from battledress to something cooler and more effective for the summer months. Khaki drill, used in North Africa, was too bright a colour for use in the green and brown hills of Umbria. They chose khaki shirts and dark green denim trousers, covered by para-type smocks – this combination proved to be very efficient.

It is interesting to note that in engaging with Italian campaign historians the author discovered that some had mentioned their belief that these smocks were a variation of a regular airborne Denison smock as quoted by Curtis.

Similarly, an account from Harry Green of 2nd Coldstream Guards quoted in Quilter's *No Dishonourable Name*, again suggests an adoption or choice in lieu of an order, stating that:

For three days after the battle of Piccolo the battalion remained resting in that area. There had been a number of casualties which required replacing …. The weather was now very hot and we were, of course, wearing KD. This form of dress did not prove to be very good camouflage in Italy and so the 1st Guards Brigade adopted the following order of dress for battle: American khaki shirts, denim trousers and, on top of that, a camouflaged smock.[76]

Curtis reports that S Coy was wearing battledress while Green recounts that 2nd Coldstream Guards 'of course' were wearing khaki drill on account of the hot weather. This is interesting as it might be expected that all troops within the same battalion would be wearing the same uniform. However, there are no orders stipulating dress in any of the battalion War Diaries during this period. I would surmise that this is likely due to the speed and dynamism of the advance at that time. Furthermore, there are no references to the smocks whatsoever within the 2nd Battalion Coldstream Guards War Diary equivalent to those of the 3rd Battalions of the Welsh and Grenadier Guards.[77]

We know from dress entries within other battalion War Diaries (as evidenced above) that uniform was predominantly ordered rather than, as it appears, chosen or adopted despite the lack of any specific dress entries within the War Diaries at the time.

Given the corroboration of accounts made by Green and Curtis it is likely that they were issued to 2nd Battalion Coldstream Guards immediately following the battle for Monte Piccolo. Therefore, the author does not believe that they were worn by 'S' Coy or by the Coldstream Guards during the battle.

Terence Cuneo's well-known painting depicting Company Sergeant Major T. Brown of S Coy, Scots Guards rallying the guardsmen against the 1st German Parachute Regiment holding the summit of Monte Piccolo, portrays Guardsmen wearing smocks to the left foreground.[78] This action of 28 May 1944 won CSM Brown the Distinguished Service Order.

It is likely that Cuneo undertook research and/or interviews with those who were present and thus the depictions of the garment in the final work can almost guarantee the memory of the smocks for the period in general; but perhaps not at this individual action by the troops depicted.

CAMOUFLAGED FIST

EVIDENCE, PHOTOGRAPHS AND CHRONOLOGY

No other record of the smocks appear in the narrative throughout June although it can be assumed, with some degree of certainty, that they were used by 1st Guards Brigade, during the swift advance through Lazio and Umbria and at the battles for Perugia and Monte Pacciano thereafter.

The next mention of the garment is made by Alex Bowlby of 2nd Rifle Battalion, 61st Brigade. In his memoirs, Bowlby, on or near the 1 or 2 July 1944, states that:

> At a wooded harbour area near Lake Trasimene everybody was issued with green camouflaged smocks. Our pale khaki drill, excellent camouflage in the desert, now stuck out like a range target. German snipers had picked off so many men – two of them officers within our 1st Battalion (*sic*, 2nd Battalion), had been contemporaries of mine at Radley – that G.H.Q. [General Headquarters] ponderous 'Think Machine' had belatedly decided on a variation of the German camouflage suit, something the Germans have been wearing for years. The smock certainly gave us a sense of protection and in a curious way mine made me feel I had turned professional.[79]

The term *'green camouflaged smocks'* used by Bowlby is interesting. As stated in Chapter 4, there were five colour variations of the print in use by 1944. Both the items held by the author and by Daniele Piselli are of the greenest shade.

The 2nd Battalion Rifle Brigade War Diary indicates the location of the harbour area for 1 and 2 July in the 'Daily Situation at Nightfall' report at map reference W5081.[80] The 10th Battalion Rifle Brigade War Diary corroborates the location as, '1 + 2 [July] After relief in CORCIANO by 2/4 Gurka Rifles (*sic*), harboured for 2 days in wooded area PALAZZI W.5082 (see map covering Lake Trasimene).'[81]

It should be noted that in his account, Bowlby states he was a member of 1st Battalion. He goes to great efforts to disguise his unit in his memoir, but there was no 1st Battalion in 61st Brigade. Cross referencing the events he recounts with the War Diaries of the Rifle Battalions of 61st Brigade it can be deduced, unequivocally, that he was a member of 2nd Battalion Rifle Brigade. He later describes a story told to him by a fellow rifleman in preparation for the King's parade in Arezzo which is relevant to the use of blanco and camouflage overall:

> They pulled us out of the line … and made us scrub our equipment. You know what it was like when we left Egypt? It was like that only whiter. God knows how long it'll take to get khaki again – the Teds'll see us for miles.*[82]

An accompanying footnote to the comment is given by Bowlby (marked in his memoir and above with a star*) as follows:

> *At Taranto we had blancoed our equipment every day for a fortnight. Only then had it become khaki coloured. Whitish equipment worn over a camouflage smock was the sort of target a sniper dreamt of.

As a note, 'Teds' is a nickname for the Germans derived and shortened from the Italian word (masculine) for German – *Tedesci*. This was a common nickname used and consistently appears in first-hand accounts.

Bowlby also comments, with some disdain, upon the 'ponderous' lack of innovation on behalf of GHQ on not providing a suitable garment akin to that that Germans had been using for some time. This likely refers to the German *Zeltbahn 31* as issued to every infantryman, which could be fashioned into a smock of sorts. Indeed, the use of camouflage uniform garments by the Germans, while certainly not common (outside of the German Paratroopers being encountered) was certainly more widespread compared to the Commonwealth Forces. It would have likely been unknown to Bowlby that such smocks had been available within 6th Armoured Division from May 1944. This statement also implies that Bowlby had also not seen them being worn by the men of 1st Guards Brigade either.

The accounts given by Green, Curtis and Bowlby triangulate and reinforce the driver for the use of the smocks in so far that the pale, likely sun-bleached, khaki drill order and 37 pattern webbing was not suitable for the terrain being encountered and was likely causing unnecessary casualties.

EVIDENCE, PHOTOGRAPHS AND CHRONOLOGY

Detail of Map Sheet 122 (1:100,000) Perugia (GSGS 4164 series) reproduced by 49 Survey Company S.A.E.C (South Africa Survey Company) April 1944. This illustrates the operational area for 6th Armoured Division during late June and early July 1944.

As an aside, the 61st Brigade War Diary records the King's visit:

> 26 [July], 0830, Visit of H.M. The King. The route near L'OLMO at 227277 was lined by 500 men from the Bde: owing to operational commitments the Bde Comd and the staff with the exception of the Staff Capt were unable to attend. Lt. Col R.A. FYFFE, M.C. represented the Comd and 7 RB provided 330 men, 2 RB and 10 RB 70 men each and Bde HQ and Sigs Sn 20 between them.[83]

A *Sit-rep* document from the same day within the 1st Guards Brigade War Diary also states:

> Large portion from every unit in the Brigade were inspected this morning by His Majesty the King, on the road between OLMO and the bridge at 231279.[84]

July 1944 offers by far the most well documented evidence of use from both eyewitness accounts and the photographic record.

An entry within the personal diary of Major Dalrymple from 'S' Company, Scots Guards on 16 July states that on a forward position south of Arezzo on Monte Lignano (that had been contested for a fortnight and was finally taken by 1st Guards Brigade):

> I got separated from my pack and was only dressed in a sweatshirt and trousers with a camouflage smock over the top.[85]

This key diary entry provides certainty that field officers also used the smocks.

Bowlby also makes reference to their use during the fighting for Monte Lignano, albeit 61st Brigade had been fighting there since 6 July:

> I ran into an emergency stretcher-party in need of a fourth man. They were carrying a wounded rifleman in a camouflage jacket.[86]

No.2 Army Film and Photo Section of the Army Film and Photographic Unit were present in the Arezzo area on 16 and 17 July. The 1st Guards Brigade War Diary notes on 17 July the presence of 'press photographers' with an accompanying comment that 'it pays to pander to the press.'[87] Some 80 years later, the author is grateful for the welcome provided by the brigade to the war photographers as the frames taken by Sergeants Best, McConville and Menzies are crucial in recording the use of the smocks in the field over 12 important photographs.

EVIDENCE, PHOTOGRAPHS AND CHRONOLOGY

Detail from Road Map Sheet 13 (1:200,000) printed by the U.S. Army Map Service in 1943. It illustrates the operational area for 6th Armoured Division during early and mid-July 1944.

EIGHTH ARMY. FALL OF AREZZO NA16932. For Story see NA16931. Men (of 10 R.B.) talking to civilians outside Arezzo. This infantryman found the right type of headgear to protect him from the hot Italian sun as he marched in pursuit of the enemy. SECRET: 6th Armd Div. Arezzo Taken by Sjt McConville. 16.7.44. (Imperial War Museum, photograph & caption)

Entries within the 61st Brigade War Diary[88] and those of the individual Rifle Battalions certify that these photographs were taken along the unpaved Route 71 at the L'Olmo Pass towards Arezzo through the Welsh Guards lines. Most of the men are wearing khaki drill complete with netted helmets with added scrim. Emanuele Moretti, a local historian, has confirmed that the large straw sun hat worn by one of the riflemen is of the style still used by farmers within the region today. Close inspection of the photograph below shows that he is also wearing a beret beneath it. Note the lighter smock camouflage print (probably faded) and the mixture of blancoed and scrubbed/sun-bleached webbing. Also note the detail of the tie tabs of the smock. The rifleman also appears to be wearing khaki drill trousers while some of the others within the photograph are wearing denim.

The NCO is wearing a smock with a more defined and contrasted print. The position of the pattern is almost identical to that owned by the author. It also appears that his smock has been adapted to enable the epaulettes of the khaki drill shirt to be worn *through* and over the smock. This has presumably been achieved by making two incisions in each side of the garment. Later images evidence that this

EVIDENCE, PHOTOGRAPHS AND CHRONOLOGY

modification was commonplace within 10th Battalion Rifle Brigade. He is carrying a U.S. Lend Lease M1928 Thompson.

The NCO is shown wearing a U.S. pattern herringbone twill khaki drill bush jacket and carrying an M1A1 Thompson. See Chapter 8 for a modern reconstruction of this NCO. Contrary to popular belief, M1A1 Thompsons were widely used by British and Commonwealth Forces (particularly Canadians) from the outset of the invasion of Italy. While the weight reduction of the M1A1 over the M1928 (resulting from manufacturing efficiencies to reduce unit cost) was likely appreciated by the troops, it is said that the latter was the easier and more accurate model of the two to shoot. This is attributed to the combination of the effectiveness of the Cutts Compensator (a device fitted onto the end of the barrel) which reduced muzzle climb during firing and the faster rate of fire of the M1928 and improved recoil harmonics. The Cutts Compensator was removed on the M1A1 as a manufacturing efficiency and cost reduction.

CAMOUFLAGED FIST

EIGHTH ARMY. FALL OF AREZZO NA16937. Riflemen of the 10 R.B. were the first infantrymen in the town. Some of them are seen with civilian admirers walking through the town. SECRET: 6th Armd Div. Arezzo Taken by Sjt McConville. 16.7.44. (Photograph courtesy of Neil Powell, www.battlefieldhistorian.com. Imperial War Museum, Caption NA16937)

EIGHTH ARMY. FALL OF AREZZO NA16931. Arezzo, the town that had been sternly defended by the Germans for over a fortnight, fell to the units of 6 Armd Div. on the morning of 16 July. Men (of the 10 R.B.) talking to civilians outside Arezzo. SECRET: 6th Armd Div. Arezzo Taken by Sjt McConville. 16.7.44. (Imperial War Museum, photograph & caption NA16931)

This photograph is again believed to be taken on or near Route 71 at the L'Olmo Pass and shows three riflemen sitting with eleven Italian civilians. A Bren Gunner and NCO (with Thompson) can be seen in the background also. The three riflemen amongst the group are wearing camouflaged smocks. Again, we see that they have been modified to enable shirt epaulettes to be exposed while the smock is being worn. The rifleman nearest the camera is wearing the khaki motorised infantry beret and one of the men's Indian netted helmet is being worn by the civilian to the far right. The rifleman to the centre facing the camera has presumably given his helmet to the boy to the left. It appears that the helmet has been covered in fabric in lieu of a net. While it is difficult to discern in this individual photograph, other photographs taken on 16 and 17 July show the use of what seem to be fabric camouflage helmet covers. It is possible that this fabric is M1929 *Telo Mimetico* worn *lato carne*,[89] that is with the obverse (not printed or extremely subdued camouflaged side) exposed but this cannot be confirmed.

On the same day, Sergeant Best also took the photograph of the 3rd Battalion Welsh Guards that is discussed, within the preface.

EIGHTH ARMY. AREZZO NA16966. (No.1 Coy, 2nd Bn Welsh Guards) resting beside Route 71 after taking one of the hills west of Arezzo. SECRET: 6 Armd Div. Arezzo. Taken by Sjt Best 16.07.44. RELEASED.[90] (Photograph courtesy of Neil Powell, www.battlefieldhistorian.com. Imperial War Museum, Caption NA16966)

EVIDENCE, PHOTOGRAPHS AND CHRONOLOGY

The 1st Guards Brigade War Diary contains a 'Detailed Intentions – Night 15/16 July' report outlining the objectives of the attack of 15 July, the night preceding the day this photograph was taken as follows:

3 WG will pass through 2 COLDM GDS at VAL DI ROMANA, or at the point which 2 COLDM GDS have reached and will:
(i) Clear PARADISO
(ii) Move on to the Il CASTELLARE with object of seizing and holding this feature
(iii) Block rd area 259297
(iv) Continue to hold PARADISO.

RESPONSIBILITY FOR HOLDING GROUND 3 WG
PARADISO – rd 259297 – IL CASTELLARE[91]

The 3rd Battalion Welsh Guards War Diary gives additional detail of the action:

15 [July] – Bn left for PULICIAN 2624 at 0045hrs and had occupied buildings by 0330 hrs. Breakfast eaten at 0500hrs. Orders to move up to SAN ANDREA came at 0800 hrs and Bn moved into houses. Bn HQ overlooking area towards AREZZO. Bn moved forward 1200 hrs, following up the GREN GDS and COLDM GDS. Contact made with 3 G.G. & 2 C.G. 1 Coy attacked at 2300 hrs, Pt 482 & Pt 516, capturing them without opposition. A very tiring day, men were very thirsty.

16 [July] – 3 and 4 Coys passed through 1 Coy and, after arty conc[entration] which came down on 1 Coy killing 1 Sjt and wounding 2 Sgts, captured PARADISO and Convent features. 1 Coy went on and captured EL CASTELARE by 0500 hrs. Patrol activity by us. One SCHUH mine caused three casualties. One enemy PW deserter in plain clothes was captured.[92]

This has enabled the exact location of the photograph to be identified as being a short distance from the junction of Route 71 and a track leading down the hill from Villa Paradiso within the L'Olmo Pass west of Arezzo.

Given the exact known aspect and location – and thus the position of the sun – and the fact that the men remain in battle order complete with haversacks and helmets, it is the author's belief that this was taken during the late morning 16 July. Note the mixed use of unblancoed/scrubbed webbing and the face veil worn around the head by the Bren gunner. Also note the brass leek cap badge on the khaki motorised infantry beret of the guardsman to his right. All three images taken by the Photographic Unit on 16 and 17 July show the riflemen of the section carrying SMLEs.

This photograph features in both Brutton and Ellis's titles. Ellis captions this photograph as:

Men of No.1 Company, 3rd Battalion Welsh Guards resting during the battle for Arezzo. It was the height of the Italian summer and the men were in the fighting order worn in hot weather; canvas trousers, American pattern shirt, cap comforters and, in most cases, camouflage smocks. The Non-Commissioned Officers include Sergeant G. James, Lance Sergeant R. Davis and Lance Corporal H. Lewis.[93]

As stated in the preface, and on a personal note, it is disappointing that Ellis fails to mention, or incorrectly attributes the name of the NCOs, missing out the author's great grandfather (Glyn Spowart). It is believed that the Sergeant sitting centre background is the same person shown in the group photograph in Chapter 3, back row second from left (now clean shaven). Notwithstanding Ellis's mistake in misattributing the author's great grandfather, it is possible that this man may be identified as either Sergeant James or Lance Sergeant Davis.

The use of Indian helmet nets and scrim can be seen in four of the three discernible helmets in the photograph. It also appears that the helmets have been painted in a light (possibly green) colour and augmented with scrim to further improve camouflage. The net bottom left appears to be of a tighter British or Canadian woven pattern.

EVIDENCE, PHOTOGRAPHS AND CHRONOLOGY

A British Mk II Helmet, dated 1942, with a heavy, rough camouflaged shell and 1942 dated size 7 liner. The helmet came complete with an Indian pattern net along with a solid provenance to the Italian campaign

On the following day, 17 July, Sergeant Best took two further sequences of photographs of the No.1 Company Welsh Guards, from both the front and rear.

A 'Sit-Rep & Intelligence Report' dated 18 July 1944, recounting the previous days' activity, within the 3rd Welsh Guards War Diary[94] provides an approximate area for these photographs:

> The br PONTE A BURIANO was found unblown but prepared for demolition and one German Sapper was captured there. He said that he had been ordered to delay his demolition until further troops crossed the bridge from the SOUTH. Yesterday the adv was continue (*sic*) up the four roads leading NORTH from this br. There was no spectacular adv; an O.P. was est at 205387 an (*sic*) armour penetrated to within half a mile of MELICIANO 2139. Contact was est with both enemy A.Tk. guns and infantry.

CAMOUFLAGED FIST

EIGHTH ARMY. AREZZO NA16989. Men (of No.1 Coy, 3 Bn Welsh Guards) moving up to new positions on a hill near Arezzo. SECRET: 6 Armd Div. Arezzo. Taken by Sjt Best 17.07.44. (Imperial War Museum, Photograph & Caption NA16989)

Note again the light-coloured paint applied to the helmets and the use of scrim. Also see how the guardsmen second and third from left have suspended their helmets from their water bottles. All of the men are in full battle order complete with haversacks and gas capes. A number of the guardsmen are also carrying General Service Spades in addition to their personal entrenching tools, this is different to the practice undertaken by 10th Battalion Rifle Brigade on the same day. Again, the Bren gunner second from left appears to have covered his helmet with a fabric cover.

EVIDENCE, PHOTOGRAPHS AND CHRONOLOGY

This second frame taken by Sergeant Best features another section of Welsh Guardsmen. It appears that the corporal in the foreground has a camouflaged fabric covered helmet. It is impossible to tell whether this is *Telo Mimetico* or merely painted fabric. Also note the dual bandoliers being worn by some.

On the same day Sergeants McConville and Menzies take a six-frame sequence of a patrol of C Company, 10 Rifle Battalion.[95] Once Arezzo had been taken, the riflemen raced hard to seize the Arno bridges to the north and west.[96]

EIGHTH ARMY. AREZZO NA16990. Men (of No.1 Coy, 3 Bn Welsh Guards) moving up to new positions on a hill near Arezzo. SECRET: 6 Armd Div. Arezzo. Taken by Sjt Best 17.07.44. (Imperial War Museum, photograph & caption NA16990)

CAMOUFLAGED FIST

EIGHTH ARMY. MOTORISED INFANTRY PATROL. NA16873. Motorised infantry at the patrol rendezvous. SECRET: 6 Armd Div. N. of Arezzo. Taken by Sjt McConville 17.07.44. (Imperial War Museum, Photograph & Caption NA16990)

The first photograph from the sequence shows a moving halftrack while a number of officers and other men look on. It is interesting to note that most are wearing the khaki beret for motorised troops with the exception of two riflemen wearing service caps. Almost all of the men within the photograph, including those within the halftrack, are wearing camouflage smocks. Both men in the left foreground appear to be officers on account of their footwear (see below). The first is believed to be a junior officer, perhaps a lieutenant, on account of his wearing of basic pouches, being armed with an M1928 Thompson but carrying a pair of binoculars. He also appears to be wearing denim trousers.

The second from left, likely a more senior officer, is wearing khaki drill, and carrying binoculars and a *board, Map, No.2 Mk 1* (see photographs in Chapter 8). Note that his smock has also been modified to enable the epaulettes to be exposed. Another man is obscured behind the officers and in the right background a rifleman can be seen wearing goggles.

EVIDENCE, PHOTOGRAPHS AND CHRONOLOGY

This photograph is important as it evidences wear of the smock in field conditions by officers which tallies with the account provided by Major Dalrymple of S Coy of the Scots Guards.

The rifleman to the right foreground, perhaps an NCO, offers one of the most unrestricted views of the print pattern of the smocks of all available contemporary photographs. The (reverse) 'L shaped' stitching can be seen to the bottom right of the garment enabling this to be positively identified as a Type A garment (see

Chapter 7). He is also wearing a pair of goggles around his neck as identified from the distinctive strap, likely owing to the dusty conditions caused by the summer heat.

EIGHTH ARMY. MOTORISED INFANTRY PATROL. NA16874. Infantrymen of the R.B. on daylight patrol. SECRET: 6 Armd Div. N. of Arezzo. Taken by Sjt Menzies 17.07.44. (Imperial War Museum, Photograph & Caption NA16874)

The next frame shows the riflemen marching. Unfortunately, the author was unable to obtain the 'caption sheet' referred to by the Museum that accompanied these images for the 'story' behind them. Again, there is a mix of netted helmets with and without scrim in addition to the wearing of berets. Notable is the fifth man from right in the column who is carrying his helmet with the strap suspended over his left basic pouch. It appears that the men are predominantly wearing khaki drill shirts with denim trousers and are carrying SMLE rifles and G.S. spades. Later photographs in the same series show some riflemen carrying No.4 rifles. There are no images known

to the author showing the use of No.4 rifles by the guardsmen of 1st Guards Brigade in 1944 – aside from the special issue No.4T sniper rifles.

Photographs of the Welsh Guards in April 1943 near Kairouan in Tunisia evidence that they had been issued with No.4 rifles. This is unexpected as one would expect that given the earlier issue of No.4s they would have been retained for Italy as a more recent weapon.

Closer scrutiny of the image reveals that the rifleman to the left is wearing a jack-knife lanyard tied around his chest above his basic pouches. His belt also appears to have been blancoed.

The smock worn by the NCO to the far left (see above) carrying an M1928 is interesting as it is the only example photographed where the orientation of the print is different – horizontal rather than vertical (see Chapter 7).

EVIDENCE, PHOTOGRAPHS AND CHRONOLOGY

EIGHTH ARMY. MOTORISED INFANTRY PATROL. NA16875. For story see caption sheet. Infantrymen of the R.B. on daylight patrol. SECRET: 6 Armd Div. N. of Arezzo. Taken by Sjt Menzies 17.07.44. (Imperial War Museum, Photograph & Caption NA16875)

The third frame of the series features a similar scene albeit with different members of the company and taken from behind the column rather than ahead of it. Note that few of the men are carrying their personal issue entrenching tools but many are carrying G.S. spades and picks.

The company U.S. Lend Lease No.48 wireless set can also clearly be seen in the detail. It is possible the operator behind the rifleman carrying the set is the company or a platoon commander. He is not wearing anklets but does appear to be wearing ammunition boots and basic pouches. His netted helmet is suspended over the signals pouch that he is carrying at the small of his back.

CAMOUFLAGED FIST

EIGHTH ARMY. MOTORISED INFANTRY PATROL. NA16876. For story see caption sheet [see above re 'story']. Infantrymen of the R.B. on daylight patrol. SECRET: 6 Armd Div. N. of Arezzo. Taken by Sjt Menzies 17.07.44. (Imperial War Museum, Photograph & Caption NA16876)

The fourth photograph features the men descending down the steep valley towards the banks of the River Arno. The north face of the blown *Ponte di Pratantico* viaduct which carries Route 69 through San Leo west of Arezzo can be seen in this photograph and this has enabled me to ascertain that the riflemen were walking in a southerly direction. This has enabled the track in the previous photographs to be pinpointed to that running parallel to the Arno.

The damaged bridge was subsequently repaired by 625 Field Squadron, Royal Engineers with a 40ft Class 40 bailey bridge between the two blown gaps on the remaining viaduct structure (one is concealed behind the Bren gunner).[97]

The Bren gunner in the foreground is carrying a Mk1 or Mk1* Bren gun and is wearing a Type A camouflage smock as denoted by the stitching to the bottom left of the garment. Note that he is not carrying his entrenching tool but is carrying a haversack.

The rifleman standing ahead of him, is carrying a non-standard, possibly locally 'liberated', spade and an SMLE. Similar to others captured by the Photographic Unit, it appears that his helmet is covered in camouflaged material. Again, it is impossible to tell whether this is *Telo Mimetico* or merely painted fabric.

The fifth image in the sequence features further riflemen moving down towards the River Arno:

EIGHTH ARMY. MOTORISED INFANTRY PATROL. NA16877. The men wind their way down into the beautiful Arno Valley. SECRET: 6 Armd Div. N. of Arezzo. Taken by Sjt Menzies 17.07.44. (Imperial War Museum, photograph & caption NA16877)

The two men in the foreground wear helmets covered in British pattern nets and both are wearing camouflage smocks. Ahead of them, to the left of the second rifleman appears to be an officer. In the background 22 men of C company can be seen moving towards the crossing point.

The final photograph of the series shows C company crossing the Arno (back in the direction of Arezzo) at the exact location of the farthest rifleman to the top left in the previous photograph.

CAMOUFLAGED FIST

EIGHTH ARMY. MOTORISED INFANTRY PATROL. NA16878. For story see caption sheet. The patrol crosses the shallow River Arno. SECRET: 6 Armd Div. N. of Arezzo. Taken by Sjt Menzies 17.07.44. (Imperial War Museum, caption NA16878. Photograph courtesy of Neil Powell, www.battlefieldhistorian.com)

Note that all of the men are wearing smocks and none are carrying personal entrenching tools.

It can be seen that another rifleman has taken over the duties of carrying the No.48 wireless set since the third photograph in the series (noted by the difference in water bottle carrier). One can't help but admire the strength, fitness and resilience of the rifleman in carrying this cumbersome wireless set, complete with webbing, weapon and pick axe in the heat and sun of a Tuscan summer.

A detailed analysis of the photograph below confirms that two of the riflemen are carrying No.4 rifles in contrast to those in earlier photographs.

Additionally, the NCO/Officer is carrying an M1A1 Thompson (the absence of Cutts Compensator and side cocking handle) which again differs to the M1928s in the earlier photographs. Note also the partially netted and painted helmet worn by the rifleman in the foreground. In the detail below

EVIDENCE, PHOTOGRAPHS AND CHRONOLOGY

the *Ponte di Pratantico* can be seen through the gap in the trees.

A month later, at Rufina in September 1944, Alex Bowlby recalled that the 2nd Rifle Battalion were still wearing khaki drill clothing despite much cooler weather:

> In the end the cold put an end to the quarrelling. We were still wearing lightweight khaki drill. Major Dunkerely [a disguised name – there is no Major Dunkerely listed within the War Diary] had already asked the Q.M. for greatcoats and had been told they were on the way up from Taranto, along with the rest of our winter kit.[98]

The next evidence of the garment appears in the first half of October 1944. Alex Bowlby, in further recounting the poor weather conditions a month later and now near Monte Orlando, states:

> It was the worst Autumn in Italy for twenty years. Rain fell almost continuously, and in the mountains it turned to sleet. The men were still in summer kit. One night a rifleman in the 1st Battalion [should be 2nd Battalion] died of exposure. Twelve others were carried down the mountain. The next day D Company got its winter kit.[99]

Henry Taylor, in his memoir, makes no specific mention of having been issued with, or wearing, smocks although he does recount the same tragic incident highlighting the lack of winter clothing and the awful weather conditions:

> The weather was atrocious: first the rain which washed away the engineer's bridges, then the snow deep enough to fill your pockets. One rifleman died of exposure near Borgo, San Lorenzo and all modern mechanised warfare ground to a halt. The battalion was still issued their summer KD uniform so cases of hypothermia increased. When a rifleman died of exposure, the request for battledress became imperative. Rumour was that requests were made for 150,000 battledress, few of which reached the frontline troops.[100]

It is difficult to fathom the expectation of fighting stubborn defenders high up in the Italian Apennines in winter with clothing designed for a tropical environment!

Bowlby recalls while exhuming a hastily buried fallen comrade for re-burial there that '[Owen] took off his camouflage smock to use as a stretcher.'[101]

This was likely achieved by unfolding the garment to its full length to hold the body.

He later states that sometime between the second week in December 1944 and Christmas day, on Monte Penzola:

> During the Christmas rest we had been equipped with winter kit of surprisingly good quality. I had most of mine on – an Artic vest on top of an ordinary woollen one, two shirts, two pullovers, two pairs of pants, a snow-proof anorak, a greatcoat, a cap comforter and a leather jerkin lined and sleeved with an American blanket. The cold got through the lot.[102]

Again, at Monte Penzola, Andrew Gibson-Watt of the Welsh Guards recalls that, 'snow came just before Christmas, and we were issued with white smocks and other good winter clothing'[103] (see Chapter 8 and Appendices I and II). He also states that the 1st Guards Brigade remained within this immediate area until February 1945 and that he had been issued with:

> …string vests and really waterproof boots. Until then everyone's feet had been wet all the time, and we had struggled with foot-powder and changes of socks to keep free of trench foot – successfully, too, because although the wet and snow easily entered the standard 'ammunition' boot, they just as easily left it.[104]

The 3rd Battalion Welsh Guards War Diary specifies the issue of specific snow camouflage in the plan to relieve the 2nd Battalion Coldstream Guards at Verro, Acqua Salata and Point 508 on the 14–15 February:

> Para 1 (j). Snow Camouflage only will be issued at MULE BASE. Boots, grooved, heel, and Boots, Boucheron, will be issued to Coys by QM 12 Feb.

TNA, WO 170/4982 (detail)[105]

It seems that upon the issue of winter clothing and the lack of reliably dated photographic evidence or narrative thereof, the use of smocks is then discontinued within 6th Armoured Division. This is likely to have been due to a combination of this new clothing, and further change in the environment being encountered plus the risk of potential friendly fire incidents.

While outside the focus of 6th Armoured Division, Quilter provides an eyewitness account from a Guardsman of 3rd Battalion Coldstream Guards, 24th Guards Brigade, 6th South African Armoured Division, that during their fight against the *16 SS Panzergrenadier Division* at Gardaletta during October 1944:

> …then I realised that only one (of two men) was a German, the man with the gun was a guardsman from the next platoon, wearing a camouflage smock indistinguishable from the German pattern; and the other, a hulking blonde caricature of a brutal SS man, was his prisoner. I nearly collapsed with relief.[106]

In addition to highlighting that friendly fire incidents were a serious reality, it also evidences the piecemeal use of the smocks between platoons and the fact that this guardsman was not aware of their use (albeit he could have been a recent reinforcement). From late 1944 the Allies increasingly faced large numbers of troops from the pro-German Italian National Republican Army of the *Repubblica Sociale Italia*, who themselves wore *Telo Mimetico* pattern camouflage clothing.

Given the propensity already discussed for the camouflage pattern to be used by SS units, and as corroborated by Quilter's account, in addition to the *Repubblica Sociale Italia* troops being encountered it is extremely likely that this increased probability of friendly fire incidents was a significant contributing factor in the discontinuation of use of the smocks.

No reliable evidence can be found, whatsoever, for the smocks' use in 1945.

Chapter 6

Manufacture – 'C' Clothing & Repair Factory, Royal Army Ordnance Corps

Upon commencing his research, the author found a common phrase almost always accompanying any reference to these camouflage smocks; *field made*. The term *field made* implies a hastily fabricated item, often made *ad hoc* with limited access to correct manufacturing equipment which would ensure a level of consistency and quality control. As such the author formed an initial theory that given the *then held* belief that the process of conversion from *Telo Tenda* to smock was relatively simple that they could have been *field made* locally by small units or perhaps by Laundry and Bath services or Mobile Stores Repair Units.

A summary of the services of the MSRUs is documented within an account compiled by the Officers of the Ordnance Services in 1950 which itself summarised all activities of the RAOC during the war:

> **MOBILE STORES REPAIR UNITS (M.S.R.Us.)**
>
> These units, allotted on the scale of one to each army, carried out "stitch-in-time" repairs, mostly to general stores of the following classes; *viz.* tentage of all kinds, waterproof covers, canopies, hoods and bonnets of vehicles, web equipment, accommodation stores, especially tables, forms and chairs, all kinds of boots (except rubber), engine chests, wooden packing cases, packsaddlery, pressure lamps, hurricane lamps and oil stoves, portable cookers, food containers and Soyer stoves.
>
> During static periods between mobile operations M.S.R.Us. did valuable work in manufacturing a considerable range of stores such as packing cases, tables and forms, simple types of engine chests, tentbottoms and duckboards, signboards and flags, sacks and various harness items.
>
> Each unit had an establishment of 1 officer and 42 O.Rs. and required no machinery apart from one "L" Type (woodwork) machine lorry and a few sewing machines.

From *The Second World War 1939–1945, Ordnance Services*.[107]

MANUFACTURE – 'C' CLOTHING & REPAIR FACTORY, ROYAL ARMY ORDNANCE CORPS

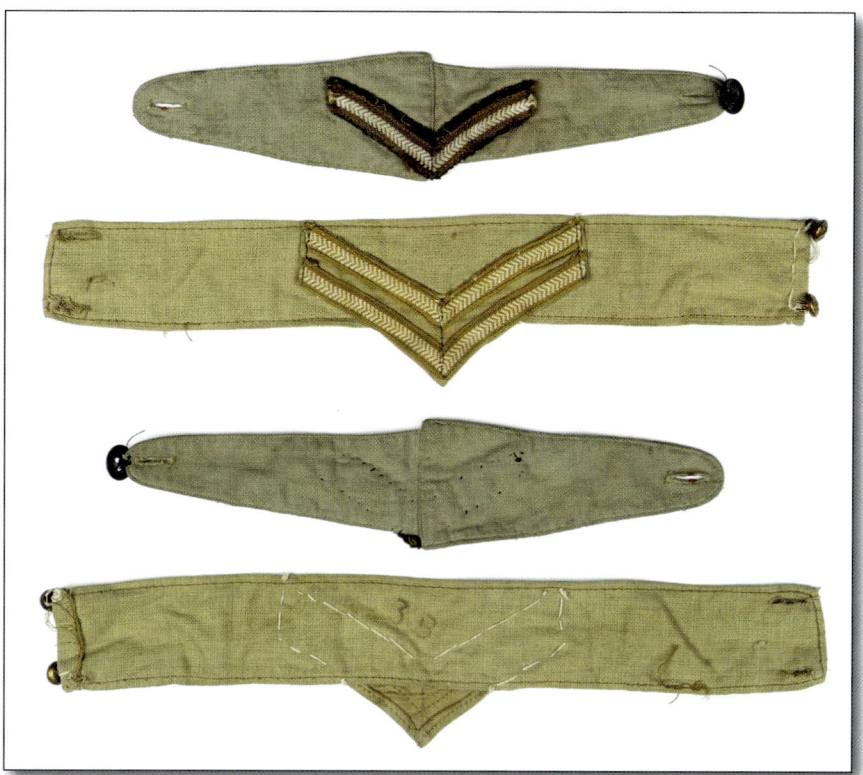

At this juncture it is important to highlight differences between the terms 'theatre made' and 'field made'. These rank brassards/armlets/armbands provide an excellent example. The top example is a field made lance corporal rank arm/wrist band made from a single khaki drill shirt epaulette. While it is functional, its fabrication is crude. The corporal armband is a theatre made item, again from khaki drill material and fitted with service cap buttons. This was owned and used in the Italian Campaign by a Corporal Mathews of 3rd Battalion Welsh Guards.[108] While both perform the same purpose, the theatre made item is machine stitched and finished with finesse by skilled workers. It is consequently of higher quality and is likely batch produced. It is probable that this armband was made at 'C' Factory.

As can be seen, the MSRUs largely provided 'stitch-in-time' repairs to general stores rather than clothing *per se*, although they inevitably had the means to repair garments, tentage and other fabrics, complete with full access to sewing machines.

> ### CLOTHING REPAIR FACTORY
>
> This unit, whose designation was a misnomer, did not repair clothing, but manufactured garments of various kinds, which were in chronic short supply from the normal source or temporarily not in stock owing to mistakes in provision, and special requirements such as abnormal sizes of battle dress or khaki drill.
>
> The unit was made up of a nucleus of military supervisors (3 officers and 70 other ranks) and over 1,000 Italian civilians, mostly women machinists,
>
> 215

> finishers and pressers. The ready availability of skilled civilians and an ample supply of many of the requisite materials from local resources, enabled the factory to produce a large supply of battle dress and khaki drill uniform, cooks' overalls and hospital clothing, and requirements for officers' shops such as pyjamas and bush shirts. The factory proved not only an economic proposition, but an invaluable asset to efficient clothing supply by virtue of its capacity to meet any reasonable requirement at the shortest notice.

Note the reference made here to a large *Clothing Repair Factory* of over 1,000 staff that, 'did not repair clothing, but manufactured garments of various kinds.'[109]

Archival research discovered the existence of a Clothing Factory War Diary within the War Office 170 CMF range,[110] this being for the 'C' Clothing and Repair Factory for the period February to December 1944.

This facility manufactured the camouflage smocks.

The first entry within the 'C' Factory War Diary provides the following rationale for its creation:

> The unit was formed in order to manufacture supplies of clothing and other necessaries for Ordnance Depots in the theatre. It was set up by Maj General Geake who selected Major E. W. Fox to select a suitable premises and machinery to enable manufacture.

… and …

> The factory commenced repairs of War Department Clothing (Grades III and IV) in February 1944 because of very heavy demands for such garments by both the Italian Military and civilians. This type of work was continued until September 1944, together with a small amount of manufacture. After September, the responsibility for repairing garments was handed over to the Italian Government and that the manufacture of garments and accessories were continued but for the British Military only. Increased manufacturing orders were then undertaken which kept the factory in full production.[111]

'C' Clothing and Repair Factory was set up by Major Fox RAOC on 28 January 1944. At the point the Factory was opened Fox was a lieutenant; he was then promoted acting captain on 9 June 1944 and acting major on 10 August 1944. The War Diary states that three NCOs were sent from No.1 Clothing Factory RAOC to assist in the set up.

The factory is documented as employing some 900 civilians, and the weekly wage bill averaged £1,150 (equivalent to approximately £42,000 per week, or £2.2m per year at July 2023 figures).

The Factory was situated on the Via Foggia, Naples, a short street near the Piazza Nationale in the centre of the city. The 'C' Factory building stands today and was most recently used as a private school. It is situated at the road junction with Via Otranto. It appears that other buildings nearby were

MANUFACTURE – 'C' CLOTHING & REPAIR FACTORY, ROYAL ARMY ORDNANCE CORPS

concerned with the supply of goods, perhaps as satellites of 'C' Factory from a reference made within the War Diary on 24 October,

> A great deal of machinery in the way of looms was removed from the premises to a factory in Via Otranto.

Additionally, the report continues:

> Extravagant claims are made by the Principo of the Insitute Technico and are referred to in the normal manner to claims & findings.[112]

While there is no further explanation of the 'extravagant claims' made, nor the 'normal manner' of the response to the complaint, this does further anchor the site of 'C' Factory in Via Foggia as the Institute Technico is sited approximately 50 metres away from 'C' Factory.

On 26 September 1944 records show that staff were being used to clear debris from the building in preparation for the expansion of 'C' Factory in support of the need to store a high turnover of large clothing stocks received from laundry units for repair. This was augmented by the requirement to store 100,000 complete sets of Grade III clothing in readiness for reissue to prisoners of war. This not only illustrates the size of the building necessary to store and produce such a quantity of garments, but that the building was also likely damaged during the intensive Allied bombing of the city and (or) the Naples uprising.

No War Diary can be found for a No.1 Clothing Factory RAOC within the CMF range, nor is it mentioned in any CMF distribution list for other RAOC factories or facilities. It is believed likely that this facility was located within the UK or in the wider Commonwealth. The fact that three NCOs were sent from there to 'C' Factory at that time suggests their experience was required to support setting up the facility at 'C' Factory and that No.1 Clothing Factory was already an established and operational factory.

The distribution lists for most communications to RAOC establishments within the CMF concerned with repair or supply of goods (mentioned within the 'C' Factory War Diary) consist of:

- Comdt. RAOC Trg. Est. [Commandant ROAC Training Establishment and contained clerks, drivers, store men et cetera]
- 00.R.S.D. 577 B.O.D [this unit repaired footwear, heavy textiles and tentage. The unit also manufactured footwear]
- 00.40 Ord. Paint Factory
- DADOS, Laundries [Deputy Assistant Director Ordnance Services Laundry Depots]
- COO, Ord. Depot, Bari

It was initially presumed that the 'C' prefix implied the presence of factories 'A' and 'B', but I now believe that this likely indicates 'C' for Central, as in CMF. No other clothing factories are found within the RAOC distribution lists within the CMF.

Consequently, 'C' Clothing Repair Factory appears to be the only factory under the direction and ownership of the RAOC capable of making theatre specific items within and for the CMF and her Allies (including Italian civilians). Entries and papers contained within the War Diary evidence that the factory was a sophisticated and self-contained twofold manufacturing and repair organisation complete with a large and skilled civilian workforce, complimented by its own military cooks, electrical engineers, drivers et cetera. A breakdown of personnel is recorded within the Diary on 26 September 1944:

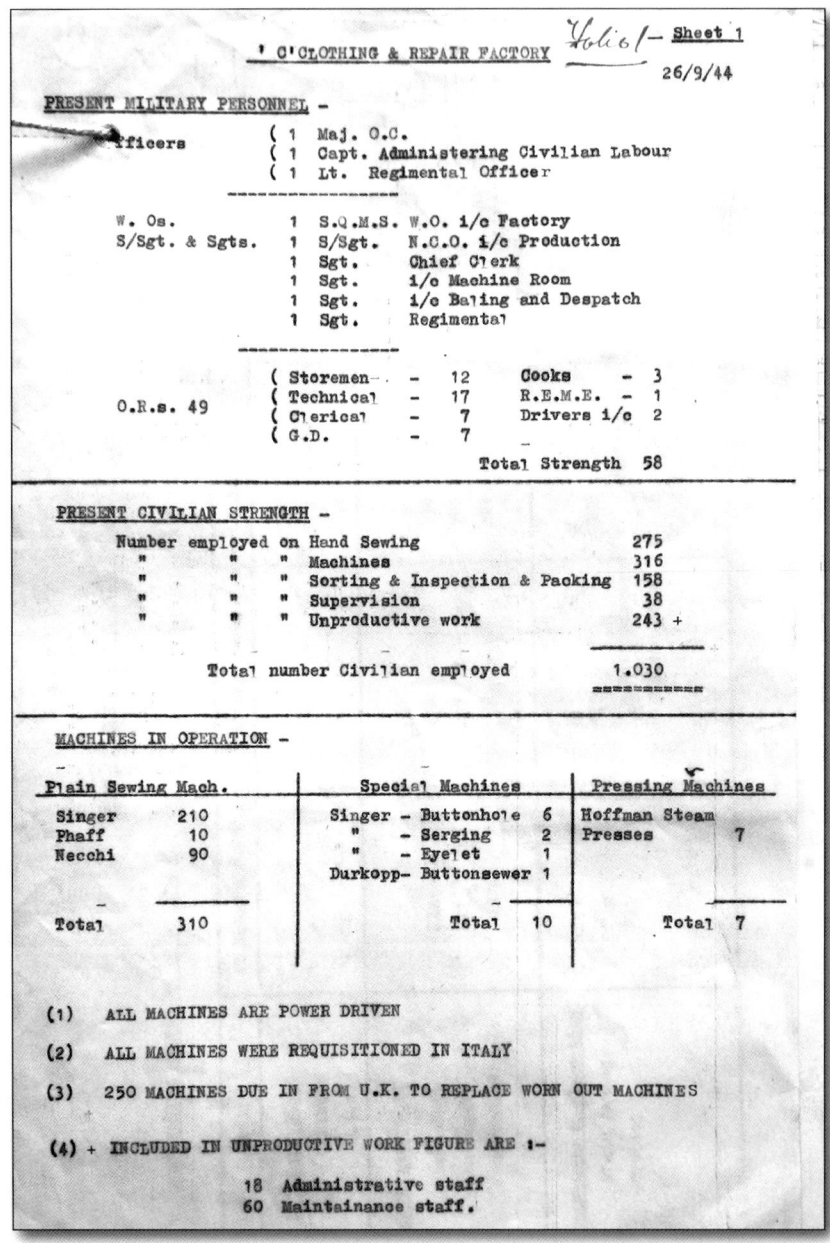

From TNA, WO170/2866[113]

MANUFACTURE – 'C' CLOTHING & REPAIR FACTORY, ROYAL ARMY ORDNANCE CORPS

A War Diary entry of 29 November 1944 states that a:

> syllabus [was created that] covers the whole of the factory's work. Students could be taken in at very short notice.

An additional letter states an order was received from RAOC command to prepare a plan:

> …for when hostilities cease it is intended to run "Refresher" courses for soldiers in existing Ord. Factories and Schools.[114]

50 students could be accommodated simultaneously over an eight-week duration course to cover various topics (see page 103). It is reasonable to suppose that elements of this course would have been taken from the package used to train new civilian workers. This further reinforces the sophistication of 'C' Factory which is able to recruit, train, professionalise and develop its work force. It also evidence of the continuing need for such a facility and the skills necessary to maintain its production into the future.

The importance of the factory to the continuance of the campaign in Italy is evidenced by a number of documented high-profile visits from (then) General Alexander on 7 October, three Major Generals including Major General Geake on 19 October (Director of Ordnance Service Middle East Command and formerly Director of Clothing & Stores at the War Office between mid–1942 and 1943) and the Inspector of Army Equipment on 28 October.[115]

Keen to ensure the continued welfare of the staff by minimising the transmission of illness to troops and workers (and safeguarding security of supply) the factory, was visited by a Brigadier Philps of DDOS to ensure, 'medical arrangements for civilian staff.' This resulted in a later order requiring, 'all employees who handle clothing after it has been passed through the mobile laundry or who are engaged in the production of new clothing should receive typhus vaccine from army sources.' A further endorsement states that 'new employees [will be] vaccinated for small pox and typhus prior to being able to handling washed clothing and blankets.'[116] To this end, 3,500 vaccines were made available to those civilians employed by the RAOC across their many sites, and administered by British Army trained Italian doctors.

It is reasonable to ask why this facility was visited by so many (very) high-ranking military officers; why it needed to develop such a sophisticated training regime; and why it was allowed to spend some £2.2 million (July 2023 equivalent) per year in wages alone? The answer is that between February and September 1944 it manufactured a staggering 286,856 items, and repaired 358,835 more. In terms of weekly input and output, during the week ending 21 October 1944, 'C' Factory manufactured 84,615 items and received 14,022 garments from laundries, along with a further 3 tons of other assorted clothing. Similarly, during the week ending 25 November it manufactured 25,125 garments and repaired a further 27,850 more, received from the laundry units. While this may represent a somewhat mundane, less exciting, element of World War Two history, the existence of 'C' Factory and its continued productivity was of paramount importance to the progression of the campaign.

Papers within the War Diary dated 26 September 1944 provide a list of garments which it had the capability to produce.[117] Sheet 4 in the document series records only 14 garments were in active production (at that time) namely:

- Bandoliers
- Battledress
- Crosses Distinguishing Hospital
- Flags Distinguishing Hospital
- Greatcoats, P. of. W.
- Handkerchiefs
- Jackets Drill White
- Labels White
- Pyjamas Cambric Officers
- Ration Bags
- Shirts White
- Shorts Khaki Drill
- Suits N/Orderlies New Zealand
- Trousers Khaki Drill

'C' Factory produced 5,982 Camouflage Smocks during the period up to 26 September, this constituted two percent of total garment production. It also enables the short period of manufacture to be identified from, at the earliest, February to mid-September 1944 latest, as the garments were certainly no longer in production by 26 September. Given the environment and landscape of the contested areas of 1943, it is unlikely that the need for a greener-coloured camouflage was identified or required at that time. This is consistent with the findings earlier outlined in Chapter 5 of the declining use of the greener smocks through the winter of 1944.

Sheet 3 of a document bundle for 26 September 1944 (see below) stipulates the garments that the factory was capable of manufacturing.

Sheet 5 accounts for the total number of each garment type manufactured by 'C' Factory by that date.

Given that there is no record of any other clothing factory within the CMF, the author deduces that 'C' Factory is likely the only *bona fide* military establishment producing camouflage smocks in Italy.

SYLLABUS OF SUBJECTS TO BE TAUGHT

Ref.Para.2 (b)

FOLIO H2 PAGE 3

1. Manufacturing

  (a) Cutting Dept.
       Marking, laying and cutting out of military clothing and necessaries.
  (b) Machine Room
       Machining of all types.
  (c) Finishing Dept.
       Hand-sewing and finishing.
  (d) Pressing Dept.
       Hoffman pressing and passing.
  (e) Central Inspection Dept.
       Inspection of completed articles.

2. Bespoke Tailoring.

  (a) Pattern making
  (b) Cutting
  (c) Fitting
  (d) Machining
  (e) Finishing
  (f) Hand Pressing.

3. ALTERATIONS and Repairs.

  (a) Grading
  (b) Repairing
  (c) Cannibalisation

4. Lectures

  (a) Factory organisation
  (b) Factory hygiene
  (c) Management of civilian labour.
  (d) Machinery and maintenance
  (e) Salvage.

5. On completion of course student would be tested by written and practical examinations.

From TNA, WO170/2866.[118]

'C' CLOTHING AND REPAIR FACTORY

LIST OF GARMENTS POSSIBLE TO MANUFACTURE

Aprons Cooks
Armlets (Various)
Aprons Butchers
" Veterinary
Bags Cash
" Mail
" Ration
" Soiled Linen ATS.
Belts K.D.-
-" Cellular
Blankets Coat Dog.
Blouses B.D.
" A.T.S.
" K.D.N/Sisters
Bags Cotton White
Blouses A.P.T.C.
Battledress
Bandoliers
Canopy Covers
Cloths Pudding
Coats Dust
Covers Cap. Scarlet
" - White-
" Epaulette Plain
" " W/Badges Rank
" Machine
Crosses Dist.,Hosp.
Curtains (Various)
Caps A.T.S.
" Cooks
" P.S.
" K.D. Patients
" Operating
" S.D.
Chemises P.O.W.
Coats Frock male
" Surgeon
Collars
Covers Mule Hind
" " Hood
" " Sheet
Drawers P.O.W.
Dresses P.O.W.
Emblems "I"
Flags Distinguishing
(all Types)
Frocks Magazine Duck
Flashes Garter
Garters Elastic
(Civ.Female
Greatcoats (Internee)
Gaiters A/M
Gloves P.D.
Gowns Operating
Greatcoats P.O.W.

Handkerchiefs
Jackets Barathea
" Bush
" Drill White
" K.D. Offs.
" " R.A.F.
" Mess.Waiter
" Serge A.T.S.
" Bed.
" Hosp.Patients
" Marker
" S.D. O.R.'s.
Kerchiefs Cooks ATS.
Kneaders Short.
Knickers P.T. ATS.
Kurtas Cotton I.T.
Labels White
Masks A/Louse
" Operating
Nets Hair
Overalls Cooks ATS.
" Civ.Female
Internees
" Denims
" Combination
" Female C.A.
" Frock C.F.W.
" N/Orderlies
" N/Sisters
" " Hatfield
Pyjamas Cambric Offs.
Patches Distinguishing
Petticoats P.O.W.
Pyjamas Hosp.
" A.T.S.Flannel
" Hosp.Offs.
" " Flannel
Serviettes
Shirts A.D.
" Bush A.T.S.
" " Cellular
Offs.
Shirts Bush K.D.Offs.
" Cell.Offs.
" " O.Rs.
" " A.T.S.
" White
Shorts K.D.
Skirts Civ.-
- Female Internees
Skirts K.D.N/Sister
" Serge,A.T.S.
Sleeves Traffic Control
Smocks Camouflaged
Suits Overall Snipers

Suits N/Order.N.Z.
Scarves Cellular
Shirts A/T Offs.
" A.T.S. P.T.
" B/D Bush
Slacks A.P.T.C.
" Div.P.T.,A.T.S.
" K.D., A.T.S.
" Serge N/Sisters
Slips Pillow.
Smocks Baker
" Butcher
Suits Mess Serge.
Trousers Barathea
" B.D.
" K.D.
Ties Cellular Khaki
" Drab.
Trousers B.D.Bush.

From TNA, WO170/2866.[119]

```
                                Folio 1.- Sheet 5
              'C' CLOTHING & REPAIR FACTORY

      Number & Types of Garments Manufactured to Date -

Aprons Cooks               12    Kerchiefs Cooks A.T.S.      1.000
Armlets Black             200    Labels Bale                10.000
   "    K.D. Union-Jack  3000       "   Cloth White         80.000
   "    M.P.             1000    Nets Hair                     550
   "    Traffic           750    Overalls, Civilian
   "    White             565     Female-Internees             400
   "    White,Train Guard 150    Overalls Cooks A.T.S.         695
Bags Cash                  24    Pyjamas Cambric Blue        6.322
   " Mail                 350    Serviettes                     48
   " Ration            20.000    Shirts A.D.                     4
   " Soiled Linen ATS.  1.500       "   Bush                   112
Belts K.D.              2.000       "   "  -A.T.S.             280
Blankets, Coat Dog.       200       "   Cellular                 2
Blouses B.D.               21    Shorts K.D. -                 224
   "    "    P.O.W.  x 18.255    Skirts, Civilian
   "    Denim               2     Female Internees             200
   "    K.D., N.S.      1.055    Skirts K.D., N.S.           1.069
   "    Serge, A.T.S.     150       -"  Serge, A.T.S.          300
Coats Dust                 97    Slacks K.D., N.S.  -        1.150
Covers Cap M.P.(Scarlet)6.500    Sleeves Traffic Control     2.024
   "       White        1.750    Smocks Camouflage           5.982
   "       Canopy          51    Suits Overall Snipers
   "       Epaulette   61.011    Waterproof                  2.000
   "       Machine        100    Trousers B.D.                  26
Cross Distinguis.Hosp.      7       "    P.O.W.  x         17.710
Curtains                   36       "    Cooks                  10
Emblems 'I'             1.023       "    Denim                   2
Flags Distinguish.REME.   700       "    K.D.                  255
   "  Red,White & Black   202    Tunics K.D.                     2
   "  Various  -           59    Voucher Packs              30.000
Greatcoats, Civilian
 Female Internees         200
Greatcoats P.O.W.  x    5.367
Jackets Bush               14
   "    Cooks             108
   "    Mess Waiter        30

x Garments marked with asterisk have been repaired and have had
  distinguishing patches inserted for P.O.W.s.


NUMBER OF GARMENTS REPAIRED TO DATE

                  =  358, 835
```

TNA, WO170/2866.[120]

Of probable interest to the reader of any book on camouflage clothing is that 'C' Factory produced 2,000 'Suits Overall, Snipers, Waterproof.' The author was not previously aware of such a garment nor has he seen, or heard of one in over 20 years of research and collecting.

Immediately prior to finishing the manuscript for this study Ron Volstad kindly shared this photograph with the author. It was published within the *Vancouver Sun* newspaper on Tuesday 12 December 1944:

CAMOUFLAGED FIST

The photograph appeared in the *Vancouver Sun* with the caption::

> WHERE CANADIANS EXCEL – Sniping, one of the 'fine arts' of war, is one line in which Canadians excel. These two Canadian Army photos from Italy illustrate some of the points of the game. In the picture Sgt Tom Evendon, of Weston, Ontario being briefed by … [clipping cut off at this point].

Ron Volstad believes that Sgt Tom Evendon is of the Seaforth Highlanders regiment. At first glance, this garment appears to be made from M1929 Telo Mimetico pattern material. However, close inspection of the coloured shapes indicates that it does not conform to the Telo Mimetico print pattern and as such is likely hand painted to mimic Telo Mimetico. This is reinforced by the damage to the paint around the knee area – this would not occur on printed fabric. Given this mimicry and the level of skill required to tailor such a garment, complete with elasticated cuffs and other advanced manufacturing processes, the author firmly believes this to be an example of the Suits Overall, Snipers, Waterproof referenced and made by 'C' Factory.

Note the contrast between the sniper suit and khaki drill worn by the briefing soldier. Also note his use of the Pattern 37 Case Map, G.S. No.2 Mk1 and a captured pair of high magnification captured German Carl Zeiss 10 × 50 *Dienstglas* binoculars. Sgt Evendon is armed with a No.4T Sniper Rifle complete with No.32 scope and his own pair of 6x30 binoculars. He is using a face veil as ahead cover and has blackened his skin as stipulated within the manual below.

As documented elsewhere within this study, there were several units using variations of the smocks throughout the Italian campaign, albeit at different times.

Of the three known surviving smocks, all three in private collections, two of the three (one owned by the author and the other by Daniele Piselli) have a number of identical features including the colour of the *Telo Tenda* material, colour and position of machine stitching, attachment of tie straps, edging, hand finishing et cetera. It is likely that this level of precise consistency between both pieces hints at them being *theatre made* as opposed to field made, and to that extent it is strongly believed that they were produced at 'C' Factory. The surviving example owned by Orazio Spampinato is constructed slightly differently, but still very similarly, as will be outlined in the next chapter.

The Diary for 'C' Factory does not contain records detailing the distribution or recipients of any manufactured garments. While it has been established that the factory had the capacity to store a significant amount of clothing and stock, it is assumed that given the dynamic nature of the campaign and the urgent drivers for requiring camouflage clothing as discussed earlier, that they were supplied directly from the factory to frontline divisions/brigades as ordered. No information regarding this process has been found by the author.

An extract from the War Diary on 30 September 1944 indicates that a private from the Welsh Guards and a corporal from the Grenadier Guards formed a part of the staff at 'C' Factory. While the Grenadier Guards had battalions fighting with 1st, 24th and 201st Guards Brigades in Italy (at various times), the only Welsh Guards battalion within the CMF was 3rd Battalion. It is possible that both the corporal and the private were from 1st Guards Brigade, and while tenuous, it is a possibility that they may have influenced their use by 1st Guards Brigade.

From TNA, WO170/2866.[121]

Given that it has been established that on 19 May 1944, 3rd Battalion Welsh Guards intended to issue 110 smocks per rifle company, each infantry battalion (at full strength) would require 440 smocks to equip its four companies, or 1,320 smocks for an entire infantry brigade. This figure does not include the need for those smocks used by officers, those lost or damaged through use, or wounding of its owner or for those whose wearers went missing or were killed in action. On that basis, the 5,982 smocks manufactured by the factory would be sufficient to equip 13.6 infantry battalions. Within 6th Armoured Division there is solid evidence of their use by all of the battalions of 1st Guards Brigade and within the 2nd and 10th Rifle Battalions of 61st Brigade. It is reasonable to suppose therefore that they were issued at brigade level, irrespective of the lack of photographic evidence and narrative for the 7th Rifle Battalion. On that basis, the two infantry brigades of the 6th Armoured Division would require 2,640 smocks in total. Notwithstanding losses, this would account for 44 percent of the total smock output from 'C' Factory.

As set out in the introduction, I am also aware of their use by the following British units:

- 5th Battalion Royal West Kents, 21st Indian Infantry Brigade, 8th Indian Division
- 1st Battalion Royal Fusiliers, 17th Indian Infantry Brigade, 8th Indian Division
- 3rd Battalion Coldstream Guards, 24th Guards Brigade, 6th South African Armoured Division
- 1st Battalion Scots Guards, 24th Guards Brigade, 6th South African Armoured Division

Should the four rifle companies within those individual battalions be issued 110 smocks each, as in 3rd Battalion Welsh Guards, this could account for a further 1,320 smocks (without replacements) or 3,960 inclusive of those in 6th Armoured Division. Following the trend of issue within 6th Armoured Division, it may be likely that other battalions of those brigades would also be issued smocks. This would necessitate an additional 3,960 smocks to equip the 17th Indian, 21st Indian and 24th Guards Brigades in addition to the 2,640 already issued within 6th Armoured Division. This is probable, given the photographic evidence of Sikh soldiers of the 8th Indian Infantry Division wearing the smocks. Should this be the case, this would require 6,600 to have been manufactured – exceeding the number made by 'C' factory. However, given the reference made by Quilter concerning the SS prisoner in the context of friendly fire (Chapter 5), the guardsman appears to be unaware of the use of the smocks by a platoon in the same rifle company! Perhaps, issue was not as standardised as one might expect and perhaps the number made by 'C' Factory was wholly adequate to account for the widespread, if sporadic, use of the smocks within formations all the way down to platoon level.

It is also possible that a smaller number of smocks were owned by each brigade and then only issued to those men actually in front line positions at that time, that is, that they were not a personal issue item. This would enable a lesser number of smocks to be required by an infantry brigade and may account for the differing issue times as in the accounts in May 1944. Furthermore, at this stage of the campaign, infantry units (see Chapter 2) were seldom at full strength so therefore would require less smocks per platoon/company/battalion. Consequently, it could be the case that the 5,982 examples manufactured by 'C' Factory represented the total number of garments produced and used by British forces within CMF. Any differences between the identical examples owned by the author and Daniele Piselli and that owned by Orazio Spampinato could be due to continuous improvement of the manufacturing processes, or variations in individual production lines or batches at the factory.

It is also plausible that some *ad hoc*, field made examples may have supplemented the numbers made by 'C' Factory. Perhaps some were indeed made by MSRUs or similar units in other Allied forces although this cannot be confirmed. It should also be noted that the garments do require some reasonably time-consuming manufacturing processes to complete (to a high standard) as will be discussed in the next chapter.

In correspondence between the author and Orazio Spampinato, he has suggested that some garments may also have been made by private, non-military enterprises and sold locally to units.

It is also conceivable that captured *Telo Tenda* stocks could have been transported to other RAOC clothing factories outside of the CMF where they were then repurposed into smocks and returned to theatre. Given the logistical challenge this approach would necessitate it appears highly unlikely that this was the case.

The smocks could also have been held centrally by U.S. 5th and British 8th Armies so it is possible that stocks were issued, used and then recalled to army stores for reissue based on need, terrain and required outcomes, although this process would be cumbersome and therefore again unlikely.

As highlighted in the introduction and in Chapter 5, accounts regarding the smocks are, at best, scant. The fact that a relatively small number of garments were manufactured and issue confirmed to less than ten battalions – nine confirmed plus likely issue to 7th Battalion Rifle Brigade – may go some way to explain this.

While the information provided by the 'C' Factory War Diary is most appreciated in the wider context of understanding these garments, the Diary raises more questions than it answers, most of which will likely remain unanswered with the details lost to history.

Chapter 7

Construction & Surviving Examples

There are three known original British smocks that survive in collections today. Two examples are known to have been sold since the mid-eighties, one by Stephen Kiddle of Pegasus Militaria and another by Phil Faram of World War Wonders Militaria. It is possible that both of the sold garments could be the same example now owned by the author changing hands between collectors and dealers, but it is likely that more survived the war. One example used by the New Zealanders is also retained in a private collection although its construction is very different to those used by British forces. It is safe to say that original smocks are extremely rare – they were made in low numbers and issued sparingly to a small number of frontline infantry units. The infantry inevitably attracted the highest proportion of casualties of British Forces in the CMF, and therefore losses of the garment inevitably contributing to their scarcity.

The smocks were worn by inserting the head through the neck aperture and allowing the garment to drape over the front and rear of the body. It was then secured in place by tying the two corresponding tie tabs of each side together. Owing to the rigidity caused by the reinforcement strips and that of the original *Telo Tenda* neck aperture (stitched closed) they create a somewhat peaked appearance over the shoulders. All images show webbing being worn **over** the smock presumably for ease of access.

It is an extremely practical garment and is easily carried – capable of being folded to a shape 23cm long by 18cm wide and 3cm thick. It will easily fit within a haversack or within the map pocket of both denim and wool battledress trousers. It is also light, at only 447g when dry.

As already outlined, of the three surviving examples two have identical characteristics, these have been classified as Type A. The other garment has different characteristics and has been classified as Type B. The differences observed in contemporary photographs in the fall of the garment over the body can be attributed to three factors; the height and body shape of the wearer, the distance of the new neck hole from the original *Telo Tenda* neck hole, the slight length difference between Type A and Type B smocks.

CONSTRUCTION & SURVIVING EXAMPLES

Size when folded to smallest possible size (.303 round for scale)

Author's Example – Type A

This example was sourced from John Boyn within the UK, who in turn purchased it during the late 1990s at a militaria fayre at Cheshunt, Hertfordshire, UK. It was found within a larger group of items containing original Italian campaign battledress garments.

While the smock shows clear signs of use and storage marks, the colours remain both vibrant and clear and overall it remains in excellent condition. As mentioned earlier, this print pattern is of the greenest colour variation available at that time. Its construction is identical to the example held within the collection of Daniele Piselli. There is no date stamping present on the underside of the *Telo Tenda* material, as is sometimes found.

In terms of its construction; two smocks could be fabricated from one *Telo Tenda*. This was achieved by cutting the *Telo Tenda* vertically through the central line and neck aperture, to create two smock patterns. The edge created by this central cut will be referred to as the cut side. Each pattern is again cut vertically along the long edge to a depth of 22cm removing the hemmed area containing the grommets and buttons and a further portion of the material. The stitching that creates the hemmed area on the shorter bottom ends (again containing the buttonholes and corner grommets) is then unpicked and each pattern is cut horizontally immediately above the buttonholes. These cuts consequently produce spare material to enable the fabrication of the reinforcement strips and the tie tabs as discussed below.

The cut side of the smock is then hemmed along the length of the garment, to prevent any fraying, in hand stitched khaki cotton thread to a width of 0.5cm to 0.9cm (variation). The three remaining edges are then reinforced with strips of *Telo Tenda* processed from the spare material described above. The edges of the smock pattern and reinforcement material strips are then folded back by 3mm upon each other and machine stitched together with thin gauge black cotton thread. This is visible on both sides of the garment. It appears that the two bottom reinforcement strips are attached to the garment first and the longer 170cm reinforcement strip is applied over them. This creates the distinctive 'L shaped' stitch pattern on the front and rear of the garment that can be seen in a number of the images within this book. The offcuts used in this example are from another *Telo Tenda* as can be seen from the different backing pattern. This provides further evidence that they were systematically made with numerous *Telo Tenda* readily available.

The remains of the original *Telo Tenda* neck aperture is machine stitched closed in the same black narrow gauge cotton thread. It is then finished by additional hand stitching to ensure closure on the exterior in a thicker gauge khaki cotton thread. The new smock neck aperture is created by cutting an elliptical hole and again similarly hemmed, as on the cut side, in the same hand stitched khaki cotton thread to a consistent depth of 0.4cm around its circumference.

Any pre-existing holes or areas of damage present have been repaired by machine stitching using the same black cotton thread as the edges. This has resulted in parts of the garment being gathered in places.

The tie tabs are constructed by folding small strips of the spare material, which is then machined stitched in the same khaki cotton thread to the hemmed areas along the centre for strength. They are then double hand-stitched to the underside of the smock with thread of identical khaki colour. Note that one tie tab was not finished correctly.

This creates a garment with the dimensions of:

- 85cm high, when halved or 170cm unfolded
- 67cm wide
- 20cm from edge to neck aperture
- 27cm neck aperture width, which is 9.5cm deep when the garment is folded and is elliptical in shape
- 28.5cm and 26.5cm from shoulder fold to centreline of upper tab (each side)
- 28cm from bottom to centreline of lower tab both sides
- 67cm × 9.1–9.8cm reinforcement strips for both bottom ends
- 170cm × 9.1–9.8cm reinforcement strips for the long uncut edge
- Tie tab length varies between 21.8cm and 24.5cm. All are 1.3cm wide

The garment also shows a repair in so far that only one side of the smock has tie tabs. The cut side has evidence of the tie tabs having been ripped out and a contemporary reinforcement repair in grey cotton at the positions of the original tie tabs has been used to keep the smock closed. The original cut edge stitching has then been unpicked, and the distance between the original location of the tie tabs has been hand stitched in a different shade of khaki cotton thread to form a continuous seam for 18.5cm. The author's hypothesis is that this damage has likely occurred in the field and been subject to an emergency field repair. This consequently prevents the smock from being fully opened out, as on the images of the other smocks held in collections.

CONSTRUCTION & SURVIVING EXAMPLES

Cut side to right, note that continuous brown print centre line which is feature present in most wartime *Telo Tenda*. Also see the original neck aperture feature to top right shoulder and the 'L shape' produced by the reinforcement strip stitching.

Reverse of previous image; cut side to left, original neck aperture feature to top left.

Cut side left, note reinforcement strips.

Underside, note repair to left mid-section of the cut side.

CAMOUFLAGED FIST

Underside. Note different material used for each reinforcement strip.

Hand stitched hem of cut side. Note difference to machine stitching at bottom.

Hand stitched hem of cut side.

Visibility of hand stitching to cut side from exterior.

Neck aperture hand stitching.

Cut side to right, see machine stitching of reinforcement strips.

CONSTRUCTION & SURVIVING EXAMPLES

Inconsistent width of machine stitching of reinforcement strips.

Further inconsistent width of machine stitching of reinforcement strips.

Reinforcement strips end stitch detail.

Bottom and side reinforcement strip hems which are folded back and fastened.

Side reinforcement strip bottom.

Detail illustrating side reinforcement strip affixed over bottom reinforcement strip.

CAMOUFLAGED FIST

Detail of overlay of side reinforcement over bottom reinforcement strip.

Side reinforcement strip to left, both bottom strips exposed.

Hem of cut side secured at bottom with two hand stitches.

Bottom and side reinforcement strip hems which are folded back and fastened.

Overlapping hem of reinforcement strips.

Crude method of eliminating holes.

CONSTRUCTION & SURVIVING EXAMPLES

Wider view of hole elimination and associated gathering.

Gathering as seen from exterior.

Tie tab detail.

Manufacturing defect resulting in one of the tie tabs not being stitched closed.

Tie tab stitching from exterior.

Detail of double hand stitched thicker cotton.

CAMOUFLAGED FIST

Detail of double hand stitched thicker cotton.

Wear to shoulder area near former Telo Tenda neck aperture.

Original Telo Tenda neck aperture hand stiched closed in khaki cotton thread.

Original Telo Tenda neck aperture hand stiched closed in khaki cotton thread.

Interior detail of original neck aperture hand stiched closed in khaki cotton thread.

Note the unpicked hem and double hand stitched repair in khaki thread. Note the gathering and grey thread (initial in field) repair following the ripped tie tab.

CONSTRUCTION & SURVIVING EXAMPLES

Hand stitched repaired area.

Unpicked seam and hand stitched repair detail.

Further detail.

Remains of bottom tie tab fastening.

Remains of top tie tab fastening.

CAMOUFLAGED FIST

Daniele Piselli Collection Example – Type A

This smock was obtained in Bologna, Italy a number of years ago. As can be seen, the construction, colouring and repeat of the pattern is identical to that owned by the author. It is also of the same greenest print available at that time and note the continuous brown print to the cut edge (right side). It features the same 'L shaped' machine stitching of the reinforcement strips and identical khaki cotton hand stitched areas. The construction of the tie tabs and closure of the original neck aperture again mirror that of the example in the author's collection. Interestingly the tie tabs along the cut edge have also been ripped out illustrating a potential production defect. This garment has not been repaired as with the example within the author's collection and can still be opened out as originally intended.

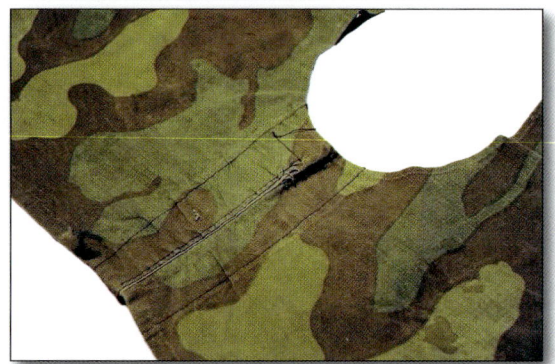

Above and right: Note neck aperture hand stitched closed in khaki cotton thread.

Reinforcement strips and tie tabs.

Orazio Spampinato Collection Example – Type B

This smock was located in Florence, Italy. Its construction is different to those held with the collections of the author and of Daniele Piselli.

This garment has been made without the removal of the bottom edges of the *Telo Tenda* that contain the buttonholes and grommets. The groundsheet has been processed to make a pattern by cutting vertically, again, through the original neck aperture and removing the remaining side edge containing the buttons and grommets. Note again the continuous brown print on the cut edge. The two cut edges have then been hemmed by machine stitching to prevent fraying. This makes the smock a little longer, and consequently when worn the fall of the garment is just above the knee (dependent on the height and body of the wearer). The new neck aperture is then cut a further distance away from the original *Telo Tenda* neck aperture than the two other contemporary examples and the drape of the garments over the shoulder is therefore different as outlined earlier.

The underside of the garment has not been processed to remove buttons and the material is stamped 'F 1934 229' illustrating manufacturing dates and codes often found on pre-war *Telo Tenda*. The tie tabs are also longer to those found on the other two examples and are machine stitched in black cotton thread.

The garment shows a number of contemporary repairs and also features a large rectangular panel that is not original to the pattern. This is a high quality and advanced modification whereby the panel being inserted has been exactly matched to the camouflage pattern print, perhaps to replace a damaged area. The colourings and wear of this panel match the rest of the pattern and therefore, the author believes that this panel was inserted at the point of conversion to smock. The panel did not come from the same individual *Telo Tenda* used to make the smock pattern as can be seen from the different *backing* material between the pattern and the panel evident on the underside. I believe that the manufacturer therefore had access to multiple *Telo Tenda* to enable this modification to be made.

Notwithstanding the complex panel modification present on this example, it is notably simpler to produce than Type A smocks. As highlighted earlier, it is possible that this could reflect production line/batch variations or efficiency improvements to increase output at 'C' Factory or point to alternative private enterprise production.

Chapter 5 shows a number of variations in the smocks worn by individuals in the photograph, most notable in the length of the garment and its fall over the shoulders. These differences are likely attributable to the two methods of fabrication evidenced between the three examples known and discussed here.

CAMOUFLAGED FIST

1934 date stamp and manufacturing/factory code.

Juxtaposition of smock against complete post-war *Telo Tenda*.

CONSTRUCTION & SURVIVING EXAMPLES

Chapter 8

Modern Images

This chapter will use modern imagery in an attempt to bring some of the contemporary photographs and stories contained within the book to life by using colour digital images. All items shown are of original wartime manufacture (unless otherwise stated) with most having direct provenance to the Italian campaign.

Nine examples of original wartime period 6th Armoured Division Mailed Fist cloth formation signs as worn in Tunisia and Italy. Most have long been removed from their parent garments. Note the differences in:
- Embroidering method
- Colour of inlay embroidering within the fist
- Width of fingers
- Size of the finger tips
- Type, shape and material used for the backing
- Attachment method (those that are uniform removed)
- Wear and discoloration

MODERN IMAGES

Plate A

This reconstruction depicts a Corporal of 3rd Battalion Welsh Guards at L'Olmo Pass, Arezzo, 16 July 1944 as in the photograph containing the author's great grandfather (Glyn Spowart), consisting of:

- 1944 dated JW & S Ltd light khaki/fawn cap comforter
- 1942 green painted and textured Mk2 helmet complete with green knotted Indian pattern helmet net,
- RZ20 German parachute off-cut used as scarf (see below for further detail),
- U.S. Enlisted man's shirt, field tailored for an officer of 4th Division (Major D. J. Lowe) complete with British fabricated epaulettes and loops in U.S. material,
- Camouflage smock
- Khaki Drill Theatre made armband owned by a member of 3rd Battalion Welsh Guards (see Chapter 5)
- 37 webbing and haversack without blanco,
- Pre mid–1941 denim battledress trousers,
- Undated wartime webbing anklets with brass capped strap ends,
- 1943 Lithgow (Australia) Mk1* Bren light machine gun.

These images show the eclectic *non-standard* mix of equipment used by the guardsmen in Umbria and southern Tuscany at this time. Despite the propensity for Foot Guard regiments to observe strict uniform regulation standards we see garments being worn that were manufactured by four different nations. Note the fall of the smock to the rear which is consistent with the stills taken from a contemporary news reel filmed in the Arezzo area, and thus almost certainly infantrymen of 6th Armoured Division. Also note the blancoed haversack in use:

125

CAMOUFLAGED FIST

MODERN IMAGES

MODERN IMAGES

CAMOUFLAGED FIST

Scarfs fashioned from parachute offcuts were universally used across all theatres of World War Two by Allied and Axis forces alike. Bowlby recalls:

> … the first thing I did was sort out my kit-bag. Apart from my books and spare clothing it contained a prized pair of crepe-soled 'desert boots', half a German parachute, a folding mirror, fifty feet of rope, a coil of wire, six cigarette lighters, spare pipes, sweets and tobacco.[122]

This example was cut from a complete RZ20 parachute canopy. This model of parachute was introduced for operational use in early 1940. Made from rayon, it was the third parachute pattern developed for German paratroopers and the first to use a camouflage pattern. It features three colours; principally a light tan, light green and a dark green.

This example measures 100cm long by 43cm wide (at its widest) and is easily folded and rolled to enable it to be fashioned into a comfortable scarf.

A MkI* Bren gun manufactured by Lithgow Australia in 1943. Following frontline service, this example was thoroughly factory repaired in 1951.

Plate B

Is a portrayal of Major Dalrymple of 'S' Company Scots Guards (attached to 2nd Coldstream Guards) as in his diary entry discussed above in Chapter 6),where he records that at a forward position on Monte Lignano on 16 July:

> I got separated from my pack and was only dressed in a sweatshirt and trousers with a camouflage smock over the top.[123]

The reconstruction consists of:

- 1939 RO & Co. Mk2 helmet complete with green Canadian helmet net, original scrim and field dressing
- U.S. Enlisted man's shirt, field tailored for an officer of 4th Division (Major D. J. Lowe) complete with British fabricated epaulettes and loops in U.S. material
- Pre mid-1941 denim battledress trousers
- Camouflage smock
- Pattern 37 webbing belt with .38 revolver holster and ammunition pouch
- Revolver lanyard,
- .38 Webley Revolver (courtesy of Lloyd Scott)
- Mk VI water bottle and bucket type holder and strap
- Undated wartime webbing anklets with brass capped strap ends
- Haversack, Officers (officers valise) complete with strap and assorted contents
- Board Map GS No.2 Mk1 complete with 1:200k Italy Road Map, Sheet 13, First Edition-US US Army Map Service 2, 1943 covering the Arezzo area
- 'Captured' German ordnance tan Voigtlander (DDX coded).6x30 field glasses complete with accessories

MODERN IMAGES

MODERN IMAGES

Binoculars were a favoured trophy of Allied troops because they were extremely expensive to purchase in the 1940s. German optics were also, generally, considerably lighter than their British counterparts being made from lighter materials in contrast to the brass construction of the latter. Their optical performance was also often better than Allied optics and generally offered a brighter image. The serial number indicates that this set was made by Voigtlander in early 1944 and they are extremely light, being manufactured from aluminium. These binoculars also retain their original strap, rain cover and optical rangefinder within the right ocular.

They have direct provenance to the 1st Guards Brigade having been 'liberated' from their original owner in the Arce area in late May 1944. The new, liberating owner had never cleaned the binoculars after the war and Italian dirt remains encrusted on their frame. Following the war, they were used by the veteran to watch birds in his garden. It is testament to their quality that they remain optically perfect and are fully usable today.

MODERN IMAGES

The officer's valise was often used to carry small items of equipment needed to perform a command or leadership role. An example of the contents can be seen here and a list of the documented items is:

Back Row, Left to Right:

- 1941 J W & S Ltd cap comforter
- Early war pattern face veil
- Army Book No.153 complete with cover and carbon paper
- 1940 dated MECo (Mills Equipment Company) Haversack, Officers and strap
- 1941 Elementary Map Reading pamphlet
- Sterling silver cigarette case 1913 hallmark
- Private purchase sewing Housewife
- 1944 Infantry Training Part VIII – Fieldcraft, Battle Drill, Section and Platoon Tactics pamphlet
- Case Pointer, Staff Mk1, a device that enabled the location of a target to be communicated and displayed to another person
- 1938 Field Service Pocket Book containing multiple pamphlets
- Field Message Book
- Private purchase D.B. Ltd No.4 Signal Torch

Front Row, Left to Right:

- BWC Artillery/Engineers/Mapping Drawing Kit
- Assorted coloured *War Utility* pencils for map copying

- Eraser
- Private purchase chinagraph crayons in leather holder
- ACME whistle
- John Players Cigarettes,
- Liberated Austrian IMCO cigarette lighter,
- 6 × 2 inch ivorene Protractor Mk 3
- 6 × 2 inch boxwood ruler
- *War Utility* HB pencil

Plate C

Depicts a Bren gunner of 2nd Rifle Battalion, 61st Brigade in Umbria, June 1944 consisting of:

- 1943 dated cap comforter
- 1939 RO & Co. Mk2 helmet complete with green Canadian helmet net, original scrim and field dressing
- Undated wartime Aertex khaki drill shirt made by R.E.H. & Co Ltd (marked /|\ and with the name Hurt)
- Undated 1942 pattern khaki drill trousers
- Camouflage smock
- Scrubbed and sun-bleached Pattern 37 webbing
- Bren gun spare parts wallet
- Undated wartime webbing anklets with brass capped strap ends
- Reproduction plimsolls
- 1943 Lithgow (Australia) Mk1* Bren light machine gun with camouflaged (green painted) magazine

This series of photographs enables the accounts provided by Green, Curtis and Bowlby to be visualised in so far that khaki drill order worn with sun-bleached webbing was not suitable for the landscape being encountered in Umbria at that time. It also illustrates how whitish equipment worn over a camouflage smock was the sort of target a sniper dreamt of.[124] The images also demonstrate how the use of the camouflage smock did go some way to mitigating the problem. In comparison with the other plates it is plain to see how the use of green denims and U.S. khaki shirts provided significantly improved camouflage over khaki drill for a greener landscape. Notwithstanding this, most images of the riflemen of 61st Brigade, as backed up by Bowlby's account and the photographic record, are predominantly wearing khaki drill.

MODERN IMAGES

CAMOUFLAGED FIST

MODERN IMAGES

CAMOUFLAGED FIST

The highly visible, and easily recognisable, upright magazines of Bren guns were often painted in Italy in an attempt to disguise the weapon, and therefore the position of the gun. As can be seen, disrupting the profile of the gun by camouflaging the magazine certainly increases the potential for an enemy to misidentify the Bren for a standard rifle, particularly from a distance. This combined with the tactic taught of maintaining repetitive single shot fire discipline until automatic fire was absolutely necessary would contribute to disguising the location of the Bren gun for as long as possible.

The Bren was key to the success of small unit actions in providing fire superiority through accurate suppressing automatic fire. Therefore, concealing the gun and its crew for as long as possible added to the impact of surprise while increasing its *killing potential* and maximising the survivability of the crew.

This represents a further, if minor, example of the innovation and adaptations made within this most gruelling theatre.

Corporal Chain Singh, 6th Battalion, Royal Frontier Force Rifles, 8th Indian Division at Lanciano, 13 December 1943. (Photograph courtesy of Neil Powell, www.battlefieldhistorian.com)

> **4. Types of fire.**—Explain :—
> i. " Repetition " firing will be employed when it is advisable to conceal the presence of an automatic weapon. Up to **30** aimed shots can be fired in one minute : these should be fired at such irregular intervals as to resemble rifle fire. In " repetition " firing the trigger must be completely released after each shot.
> ii. Rapid fire is a reserve of fire and will only be used to gain surprise effect against a vulnerable target, to cover movement or in an emergency (*see* Application of Fire, Pamphlet No. 2). Firing will be in bursts of about five rounds with only such time between bursts as is necessary to observe and re-aim. With practice a rate of **120** rounds (or four magazines) a minute should be reached. Accuracy must be maintained.

From *Small Arms Training Pamphlet No.4 Light Machine Gun 1937*.[125]

Mk. II Bren Magazine painted in dark green and stencilled to the front and rear with 2 SEC (No.2 Section).

MODERN IMAGES

Plate D

This mannequin is set as the NCOs of No.1 Company, 3rd Battalion Welsh Guards who are wearing khaki drill as in the photograph in Chapter 3.

CAMOUFLAGED FIST

The mannequin consists of:

- Contemporary wartime cap comforter, the stamp is faintly legible
- Contemporary handkerchief worn around neck
- Undated wartime Aertex khaki drill shirt made by R.E.H. & Co. Ltd (marked /|\ and with the name Hurt)
- Field made epaulette sliders featuring 6th Armoured Division formation signs (see Chapter 3 for further details)
- Tropical corporal rank armband
- Sun-bleached, blancoed and scrubbed Pattern 37 webbing
- 1940 bandolier made by R.M.M. Ltd. 4/40. Stamped with date of last fill for 17 May 1944
- 1942 dated jack-knife made by Richards of Sheffield (England)

The effect of sun bleaching, blancoing and scrubbing on Pattern 37 webbing can be seen below. Note the traces of blanco, despite scrubbing, which remain within the grain of the webbing.

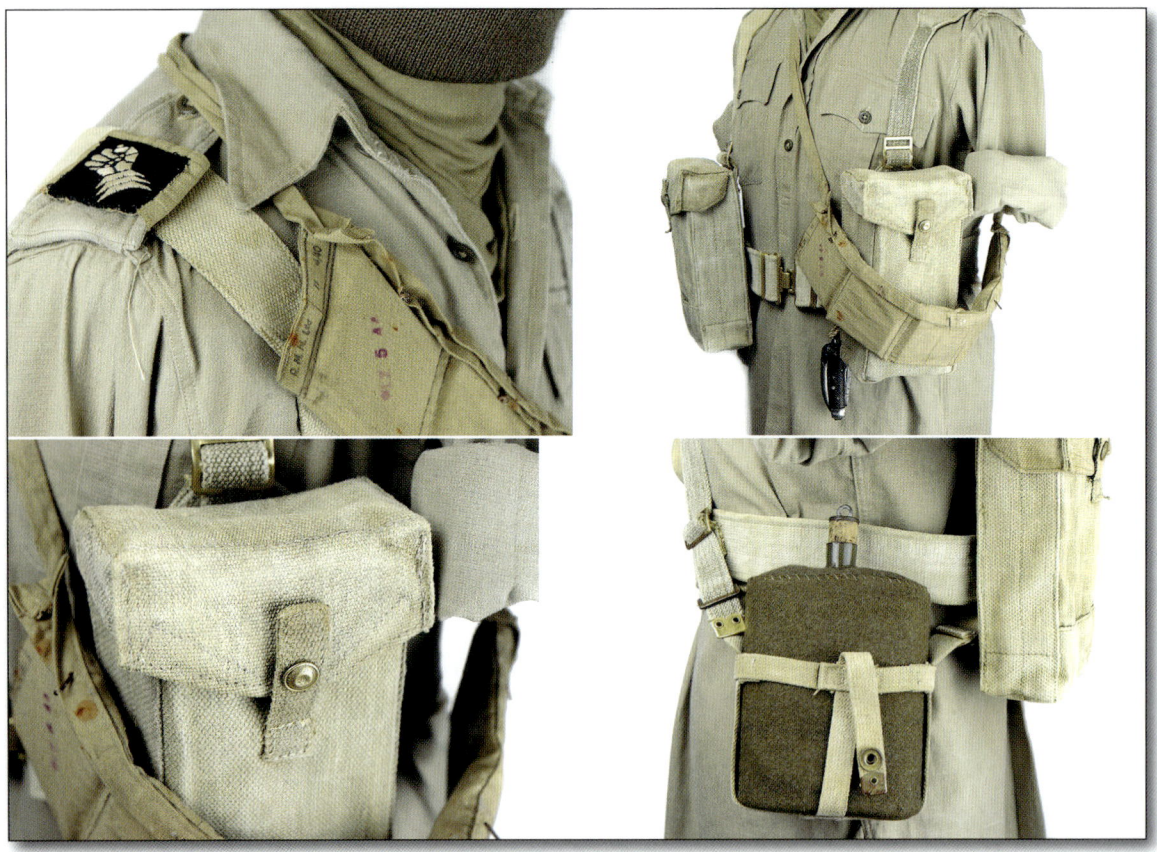

Plate E

MODERN IMAGES

CAMOUFLAGED FIST

This uniform bust illustrates the wearing of a U.S. Army Enlisted Man's shirt as used by both the men and officers of 1st Guards Brigade. This shirt saw service in Italy with Major D. J. Lowe who served with the British 4th Division. It was found in a trunk along with other uniform items and shows signs of service use and sun bleaching. It is made from the regulation mustard colour wool and features a fully buttoning front, complete with gas flap to the interior – a tab of material inside the shirt and behind the buttonholes intended to lessen the amount of skin exposed to gas.

As was commonplace, it has been theatre modified by adding machine stitched loops and buttons to the shoulders to enable epaulettes to be worn. Regrettably only one epaulette remains. The mannequin uses:

- 1943 cap comforter, /|\ stamp is faintly legible
- U.S. Enlisted man's shirt, field tailored for an officer of 4th Division complete with British fabricated epaulettes and loops in U.S. material (see inset)
- RZ20 German parachute off-cut used as scarf
- Tropical corporal rank armband
- MECo 1944 dated braces (cross straps) unblancoed
- MECo 1943 dated Mk.III basic pouches unblancoed
- No.77 Smoke Grenade manufactured in October 1943

The author has an additional U.S. shirt within the collection that was owned by Lieutenant S. M. Kirk 36717 RAOC. It is presented here with the same equipment for ease of comparison (albeit with a different wartime cap comforter which is greener in colour).

This example is less sun-faded and a slightly different shade of mustard than the example previously owned by Major D. J. Lowe. While the plastic buttons are of identical pattern they are olive-green in colour. The original gas flap has been removed. This shirt has also been modified to add a pair of epaulettes. These again have been fashioned from two pieces of identically coloured shirt material which have been hand stitched together with white cotton thread. They have then been affixed directly to the shoulder hem in lieu of being removable via a tongue and loop method of fastening as on the other example. Spare olive-green plastic buttons have then been affixed in place to enable the epaulette to be closed.

It is believed that the material and buttons used to manufacture the epaulettes often came from the removed gas flap.

Plate F

MODERN IMAGES

CAMOUFLAGED FIST

This model reconstructs the 10th Rifle Brigade NCO armed with the M1A1 Thompson photographed at L'Olmo, Arezzo as shown on the photograph in Chapter 5. Note the use of blancoed and unblancoed webbing together. The reconstruction uses:

- 1939 RO & Co. Mk2 helmet complete with green Canadian helmet net, original scrim and field dressing
- Cut down face veil for use as scarf
- U.S. Lend Lease herringbone twill Bush Jacket, marked inside Hughes 285
- Faded and well used MECo 1943 dated Mk.III basic pouches
- Faded MECo braces (cross straps) dated 1940 and 1941 (female)
- MECo 1941 dated belt with KG103 blanco
- Africa Star ribbon with 8th Army numeral/device

Many veterans of the North African campaign proudly wore the Africa Star ribbon in both the Italian and North-West Europe theatres to denote their service and experience. The 10th Battalion Rifle Brigade was a part of the 1st British Army during the Tunisian campaign but studio photographs of riflemen often show 8th Army bars worn. This may be on account of amalgamations from 2nd and 7th Battalions following the heavy casualties incurred by 61st Brigade in late 1944.

Plate G

CAMOUFLAGED FIST

Bush jackets were extensively used by the Rifle Battalions of 61st Brigade. This mannequin depicts a rifleman during the dusty months of June 1944 and shows:

- Contemporary wartime cap comforter, stamp is faintly legible
- Contemporary theatre made khaki drill neck rag scarf
- 1942 dated Albion Ltd Belfast, Aertex Khaki Bush Jacket (courtesy of Riccardo Bizzaro)
- MECo 1944 dated braces (cross straps) unblancoed
- MECo 1943 dated Mk.III basic pouches unblancoed
- M & Co. desert goggles

M & Co. desert goggles were worn extensively during the African campaign although photographs of them actually being used are rare. They were naturally carried with the troops to Italy. The frames are made from stamped aluminium which are then polished and washed with a bronze lacquer. These are easily identifiable by the distinctive 'cheese grater' vents around the rim of the frame and are distinctively different to other types of goggles used. This pair is fitted with yellow lenses, the colour of which can be changed by manipulating the frame retaining tabs which hold the glass in place. The goggles are worn by tying the two 50cm canvas straps and allowing the leather bridge joining the frames to rest over the wearer's nose.

Plate H

CAMOUFLAGED FIST

This mannequin shows a blended use of different uniform types including a denim battledress blouse, pullover and khaki drill. Combinations such as this are often found within the photographic record of those serving in Italy.

Brown coloured denim battledress blouses are extremely rare having only been produced for two years. Most of these garments were lost and abandoned during the retreat from Dunkirk where many were captured by the Germans and went on to have a second life with the U-Boat crews of the *Kreigsmarine*. The mannequin features:

- 1944 dated JW & S Ltd light khaki/fawn cap comforter
- Contemporary handkerchief worn around neck
- Undated wartime Aertex khaki drill shirt made by R.E.H. & CL (/|\)
- Wartime issue size 3 pullover (official nomenclature – 'Cardigan')
- Pre–1942 brown denim battledress blouse
- Sun-bleached and scrubbed webbing belt
- Skeleton water bottle carrier with sun-bleached long brace used as a carry strap
- Pistol lanyard used to carry whistle in left-hand breast pocket

MODERN IMAGES

Plate I

CAMOUFLAGED FIST

There is no confirmed written or photographic evidence of Aertex Indian battledress blouses being worn by the infantrymen of 6th Armoured Division. Nonetheless, as these garments have already been referred to earlier in the book an example has been included for completeness. These were introduced in late 1943 and intended to be worn directly against the skin. They would have been cool and light to wear and feature a number of innovative features including buttons that reverse fitted to prevent rubbing against the body to improve comfort. All of the buttons are of the coconut husk type often seen on other Indian manufactured garments.

This mannequin features:

- 1941 dated Mk2 brown painted helmet with British knotted net
- Sun-bleached contemporary ghost pattern face veil worn as scarf
- 1944 dated Aertex Khaki Indian Battledress Blouse
- Faded and well used MECo 1943 dated Mk.III basic pouches
- Faded MECo braces (cross straps) dated 1940 and 1941 (female)
- MECo 1941 dated belt with KG103 blanco
- Canadian Z. L. & T. Ltd 1941 Utility Pouches

Plate J

MODERN IMAGES

CAMOUFLAGED FIST

There are numerous photographs featuring the men of 1st Guards Brigade wearing U.S. War Aid olive-green battledress in 1944, particularly while 'walking out'. These garments were well received being made of a finer wool than their British or Commonwealth counterparts. They are easily identifiable in period photographs as being a hybrid of the earlier serge battledress and that of the austerity pattern, the blouse having un-pleated pockets with visible buttons. Note the green colour and chocolate brown plastic buttons.

The khaki beret was issued to reconnaissance and motorised infantry troops from 1943 onwards. There are numerous contemporary photographs in this book illustrating their wear by 3rd Battalion Welsh Guards and 10th Battalion, Rifle Brigade of 61st Brigade. This depiction uses:

- 1945 dated Kangol Khaki Motorised Infantry Beret
- Highly polished Welsh Guards Cap Badge (courtesy of Andrew Plewa)
- January 1943 dated U.S. War Aid Blouse, Battle Dress, Olive Drab (note two words for battledress)
- 1940 Binoculars. Prism, No.2 Mk2 made by A. Kershaw & Son
- Web equipment and face veil scarf as on Plate F

Plate K

CAMOUFLAGED FIST

This shows a representation of a 3rd Battalion Grenadier Guards Officer during January 1945, using:

- 1945 dated Kangol Khaki Motorised Infantry Beret with Grenadier Guards cap badge
- Contemporary face veil worn as a scarf
- January 1943 dated U.S. War Aid Blouse, Battle Dress, Olive Drab (note two words for battledress)
- 1944 dated Smock White Camouflaged
- Pistol lanyard
- Khaki Pattern 1925 webbing 'walking out' belt with KG103 blanco
- MECo 1942 pouch, ammunition, pistol
- A.C. 1943 case, pistol (holster)
- Canvas BHG Ltd 1941 Case Map G.S. No.2 Mk.1
- Contemporary woollen fingerless gloves/hand warmers

This issue of snow camouflage has been well documented in Chapter 5 and can be seen worn by men of 3rd Grenadier Guards at Monte Penzola in a photograph in Appendix II below. These garments were worn as oversuits and as an outer layer over battledress and other winter garments.

The G.S. Mk 2 Map Case worn featured here is of the less common canvas/duck cotton variety. The example shown in the photograph below was made by Barrow Hepburn & Gale Ltd in 1941. It contains three contemporary Wolff/Royal Sovereign chinagraph pencils which enable the map to be marked via the celluloid map cover (thus eliminating the need to annotate the paper map itself). Also found within is a contemporary Ivorene War Utility copying pencil along with a 6" × 2" protractor marked /|\. Beneath the celluloid cover is a GSGS 4230 1:250000 Sheet 20 Ravenna covering the area held by 6th Armoured Division at that time.

While holding positions on the Gothic Line in January 1945 the U.S. 86th Regiment of U.S. 10th Mountain Division made extensive use of snow shoes. While there is no photographic or documented evidence of the use of snow shoes within the 6th Armoured Division, given the use and availability of skis evidenced by the above referenced photograph, it is not inconceivable that snow shoes were issued too.

The illustrations below are marked 1943 on the wooden frame and the webbing heel retaining web straps made by J. & A. H. The boot fastener webbing straps were made by M.W. & S. Ltd in 1941.

CAMOUFLAGED FIST

Appendix I

Photographs – The Changing Environment

The absolutle desolation and destruction of Cassino. Postitions occupied by 1st Guards Brigade centre right beneath Castle Hill, Cassino, May 1944. (Photograph courtesy of Neil Powell, www.battlefieldhistorian.com)

CAMOUFLAGED FIST

Crew of a (M7) Priest 105mm self-propelled gun from 12th Regiment Royal Horse Artillery (Honourable Artillery Company), 6th Armoured Division, taking on board ammunition before the start of the drive to Perugia, Umbria, June 1944. Note the fertile area and olive groves– a significant change to the landscape of Cassino. (Photograph and caption courtesy of Neil Powell, www.battlefieldhistorian.com.)

APPENDIX I

6th Armoured Division near San Martino, Route 67 between Florence and Forli, October 1944. (Photograph courtesy of Neil Powell, www.battlefieldhistorian.com.) This terrain is challenging in dry conditions, it would likely be impassable during the Italian winter.

Major General Murray, Commanding Officer 6th Armoured Division, visiting some of his forward troops in the mountains in December 1944. The men are from the 72nd Anti-tank Regiment, who had been assigned to help the Royal Engineers in the task of keeping open roads and tracks during the appalling winter weather[126] (Photograph courtesy of Neil Powell, www.battlefieldhistorian.com.) Note the use of snow chains on the jeep and the white WD issue 'Coats, Duffel, Short' worn by the gunners.

APPENDIX I

An M7 Priest 105mm self-propelled gun of the 12th Regiment Royal Horse Artillery deep in mud in the mountainous Monte Battaglia sector of the Gothic Line, late 1944. (Photograph courtesy of Neil Powell, www.battlefieldhistorian.com.)

CAMOUFLAGED FIST

The carrier platoon of the Support Company of 3rd Grenadier Guards reaches the River Po in April 1945. The two carriers in the foreground are Wasp flamethrowers with their large tanks of napalm prominent at the rear. (Photograph and caption courtesy of Neil Powell, www.battlefieldhistorian.com.) A further significant change in the landscape of northern Italy, Spring 1945.

Another photograph from the same sequence as above showing a Sherman on a Class 40 Raft with a Fantail (Amphibious) Landing Vehicle Tracked to the right background.[127]

Appendix II

Photographs – Uniform Worn by Infantrymen

ITALY. THE GUARDS IN CASSINO NA15017. Cpl V. Edmunds (Grenadier Guards) of Coleford, manning a Browning machine gun at his post in the ruins of Cassino. The knocked out German SP Gun in the background is used as cover for the dugout. 1st Guards Bde. Cassino. Taken by Sgt Curtis. 17.5.44. (Photograph courtesy of Neil Powell, www.battlefieldhistorian.com. Caption, Imperial War Museum, NA15017). This photograph was taken in the remains of St Angelo School. Note the battledress worn by the guardsman.

CAMOUFLAGED FIST

A 6-pdr anti-tank gun manned by guardsmen of the 1st Guards Brigade in a ruined house overlooking a road near Cassino. Note that the gun crew are wearing battledress. (Photograph and caption courtesy of Neil Powell, www.battlefieldhistorian.com.)

EIGHTH ARMY. THE BATTLE FOR ARCE NA15664. Infantry (Welsh Guardsmen), with tank support, move up to attack Arce. Welsh Guards, Arce. Taken by Sgt Johnson 28.5.44. (Imperial War Museum, Caption NA15668. Photograph courtesy of www.battlefieldhistorian.com.) Other sources indicate that this photograph was taken prior to the battle of Monte Piccolo likely on 25 May 1944. The author believes that this photograph was taken in the evening given that the weather was reported to be very hot at this time and despite this the men are wearing battledress – perhaps as an anti-malarial measure.

APPENDIX II

Gun detachment from 152nd (Ayrshire Yeomanry) Field Regiment, Royal Artillery, 6th Armoured Division manning a 25-pdr field gun in support of the attack across the River Rapido in May 1944. Note the predominant use of khaki drill by the gunners complete with the divisional formation sign worn using epaulette slip-ons/sliders as illustrated above. (Photograph and caption courtesy of Neil Powell, www.battlefieldhistorian.com)

Lieutenant Phillip Brutton to left and Lieutenant John Davies to right of 3rd Battalion Welsh Guards. Note the wear of the khaki motorised infantry beret with an embroidered/bullion officer's leek cap badge, and also the U.S. Shirts with tailored epaulettes stitched to the shirt as shown in Plate E.

CAMOUFLAGED FIST

Lieutenant Andrew Gibson-Watt, left foreground with Tim Bolton to rear left and Christopher Scott to rear right.

An officer of 3rd Grenadier Guards uses skis to visit one of his guardsmen in a forward position near Monte Penzola during 1st Guards Brigade's stay in the mountains. (Photograph and caption courtesy of Neil Powell, www.battlefieldhistorian.com)
Note the use of the snow camouflage over trousers and anorak. While irrelevant to this photograph per se, on 22 May 1944, an order is given by the 3rd Battalion Grenadier Guards giving a direction on how goggles should be worn. This was likely in response to casualties suffered during the breakout operations.[128]

APPENDIX II

> 3. **GOGGLES.**
> Goggles will either be worn over the eyes or carried round the neck. They will not be worn on the beret above the forehead, due to the reflection of the sun.

Left: Men of the Royal Engineers of 6th Armoured Division with a bullock drawn snowplough. Note the wearing of the white 'Coats, Duffel, Short'.[129]

Below: Riflemen of 61st Brigade following the issue of winter clothing at the Gothic Line in late December 1944. As in the images above, note the use of the 'Coats, Duffel, Short'. The men also appear to be wearing sandbags over their boots for additional protection from the snow. (Photograph courtesy of Neil Powell, www.battlefieldhistorian.com)

Appendix III

Unconfirmed 6th Armoured Division Photographs

These photographs are likely Guards and riflemen of 6th Armoured Division, but this cannot be confirmed at the time of writing:

This photograph is believed to be taken on Route 6 and shows an infantryman wearing a smock without webbing walking past a disabled German 75mm PAK anti-tank gun. Without further information it cannot be directly attributable to men of 6th Armoured Division. (Photograph courtesy of Neil Powell, www.battlefieldhistorian.com.)

APPENDIX III

The caption in Italian translates as: 'The Allies also used the Italian *M29 Telo Tenda*, found in quantity in the deposits [likely depots / warehouse stocks]. Photo taken [in the] Liri Valley, May 1944. The British soldiers are wearing a camouflage smock, made like a tunic from Italian cloth.' (Photograph courtesy of Neil Powell, www.battlefieldhistorian.com.)

Appendix IV

M1929 *Telo Tenda* Booklet[130]

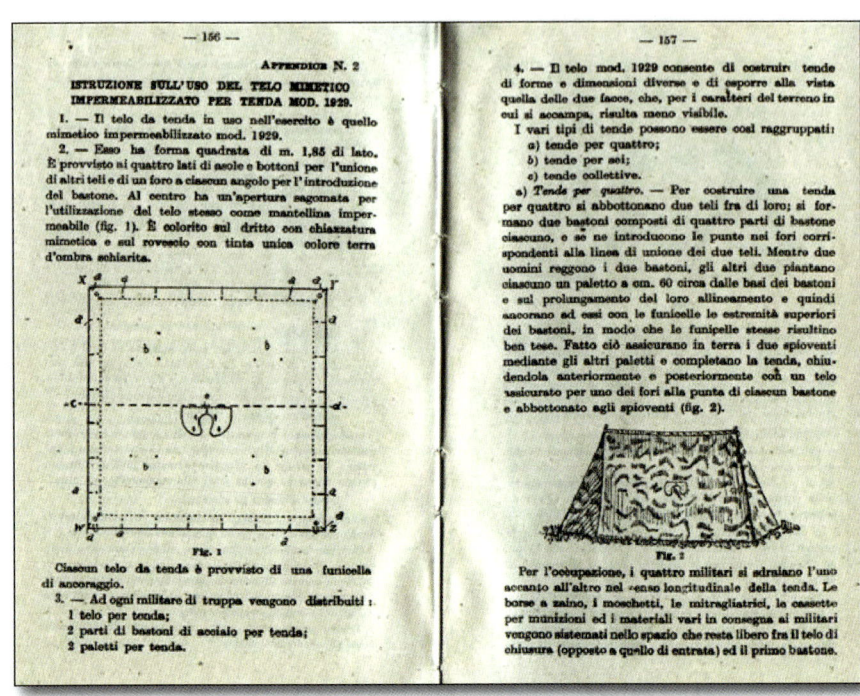

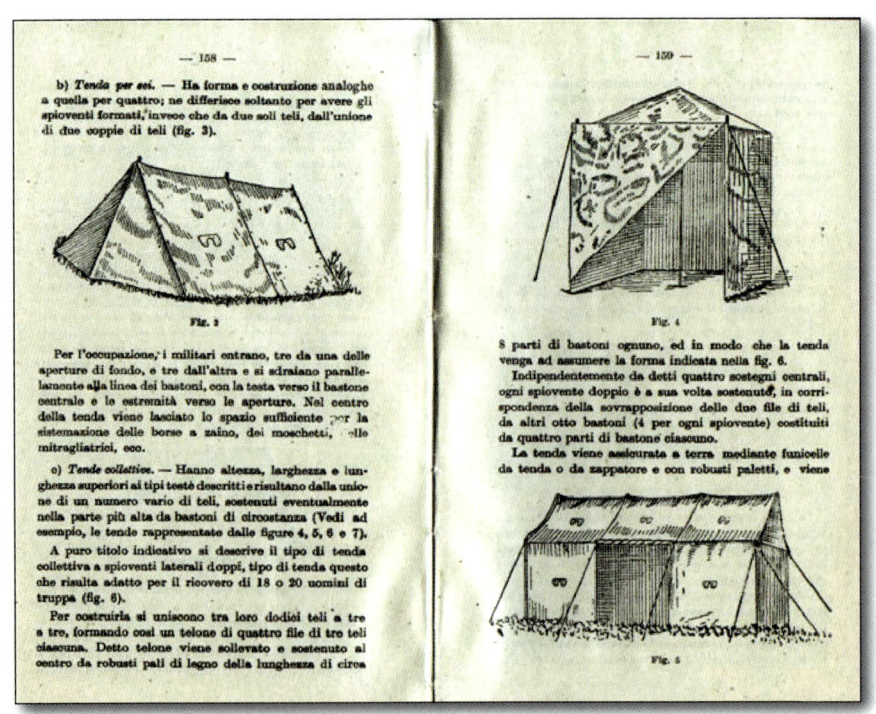

APPENDIX IV

— 160 —

chiusa anteriormente e posteriormente da tre teli che, opportunamente ripiegati, servono a costituire ingresso alla tenda.

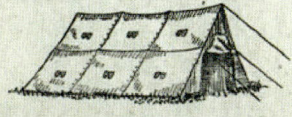

Fig. 6

Per l'occupazione, gli uomini si dispongono, su due file opposte di 8 ÷ 9 persone, con la testa verso gli spioventi laterali e le estremità verso la linea dei bastoni centrali.

Fig. 7

Le borse a zaino ed i moschetti vengono sistemati verso gli spioventi; le mitragliatrici e le cassette a zaino, ecc., vengono sistemate in un apposito spazio che viene lasciato accanto alla parete di fondo, opposta a quella che serve da ingresso.

Con la costruzione delle tende collettive è possibile economizzare in relazione alla forza alloggiata alcuni teli ed accessori che nell'insieme di ciascun reparto servono a formare tende per l'ufficio del reparto stesso, tende per sottufficiali di carriera, ecc.

— 161 —

5. — Nella costruzione e nell'uso di qualsiasi tipo di tenda, dovranno sempre essere tenute presenti le seguenti norme:

i lembi mobili che coprono le aperture centrali dei teli debbono essere sempre abbottonati e risultare rivolti verso il terreno, per impedire all'acqua di penetrare nell'interno delle tende attraverso le aperture stesse;

gli spioventi laterali delle tende debbono sempre risultare ben tesi;

attorno alle tende deve essere scavato un fossetto che convogli l'acqua verso la direzione di maggior pendenza del terreno;

in caso di pioggia battente occorre evitare di toccare gli spioventi dalla parte interna.

6. — I comandanti di corpo (o gli altri ufficiali per i quali è prescritta la tenda da comandante di corpo) usano, sia in pace che in guerra, tale speciale tenda. Gli altri ufficiali in guerra usano la tenda per 4 (fig. 2) sopra descritta in ragione di una per ciascun ufficiale. I teli e le parti di bastone di acciaio ed i paletti necessari alla costruzione della tenda per 4 da ufficiali, sono sistemati in apposito sacco custodia. In pace gli ufficiali possono essere però autorizzati a costruire una tenda con 5 teli, simile a quella rappresentata dalla fig. 4, in ragione di:

una per ciascun ufficiale superiore o capitano;
una ogni due subalterni.

7. — I sottufficiali di carriera (compresi i marescialli) si attendano a 3 oppure 2 per ciascuna tenda per 4 (fig. 2).

Nei reparti minori di una compagnia dove, pure costruendo tende collettive, non sia possibile trarre teli in numero sufficiente per costruire le tende per i sottufficiali anzidetti, questi attendano con i graduati del reparto o nel modo più conveniente che sarà loro indicato dal comandante del reparto stesso.

11 — *Addestramento fanteria* - Vol. I.

— 162 —

Non la simmetria, bensì la configurazione del terreno e la necessità di sfuggire all'osservazione aerea debbono, in guerra, consigliare la migliore sistemazione delle tende nei campi.

In relazione a tali esigenze, sarà di volta in volta ordinato dal comandante di corpo, o di reparto isolato, quale sia il tipo di tenda (per quattro, per sei, o collettiva) da costruire, tenendo presente che:

la tenda per quattro risulta la meno visibile e la più facilmente adattabile a piccole e non continue coperture del terreno. Essa deve essere perciò la tenda di uso normale;

quella per sei è la più comoda ma è solo consigliabile quando la copertura del terreno lo consente (boschi, ecc.);

quelle collettive, infine, essendo molto visibili, debbono ritenersi di impiego eccezionale in guerra, pur trovando talvolta impiego per i comandi, gli uffici, i magazzini, le infermerie da campo, ecc., ed eccezionalmente, pel ricovero delle truppe.

Anche negli attendamenti di pace occorre ispirarsi ai principî sopra accennati, e pur assicurando alle truppe il necessario benessere, debbono essere evitate sistemazioni costose.

8. — Il telo per tenda mod. 1929 trova anche impiego come:

A) mantellina impermeabile esponendo all'esterno la faccia a colorazione unica.

A tale scopo si deve (fig. 8):

a) slacciare sia sul dritto, sia sul rovescio, i bottoni dei lembi mobili dell'apertura centrale;

b) ripiegare i quattro angoli sul dritto del telo e fermarli con l'asola di angolo e con le due asole adiacenti (vedi lettera a della fig. 1), ai corrispondenti bottoni esistenti sulla faccia del telo (vedi lettera b della fig. 1).

(Per dare maggior protezione alle gambe, il telo potrà essere indossato anche con gli angoli non ripiegati);

— 163 —

c) indossare il telo introducendo la testa attraverso l'apertura centrale e disporlo in modo: che la parte cucita del riporto si adatti dietro al collo e sulle spalle; che i lembi mobili del riporto interno siano sistemati

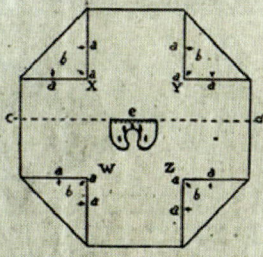

Fig. 8

tra il petto ed il telo e quelli del riporto esterno siano disposti attorno al collo e fermati sul davanti mediante l'apposito bottone;

d) assicurare (eventualmente) le falde laterali del telo contro i polsi, mediante le asole e i bottoni delle falde stesse (vedi fig. 9).

I militari a cavallo usano il telo, o nel modo sopra indicato, o senza la ripiegatura degli angoli, o con i due semilati ($Y - d$, $d - Z$, ed $X - c$, $c - W$ della fig. 1) abbottonati fra di loro, e con le mani uscenti dalle due aperture laterali superiori (vedi lettere c e d della fig. 1).

In pace, l'uso del telo come mantellina è permesso solo durante i campi, manovre ed esercitazioni: è però vietato nell'interno degli abitati.

Endnotes

Prelims

1 William I. McKenzie, *Diary of a D-Day Dodgers* (Clackmannan: Clackmannan District Libraries, 1989), p.3.
2 *The Modern Children's Library of Knowledge, Book Three* : *The World of the Past* (London: New Educational Press, 1957).
3 1st and 3rd Battalions were infantry, 2nd Battalion was armoured.
4 Andrew Gibson-Watt, *An Undistinguished Life* (Chippenham: Antony Rowe Ltd, 1990), pp.141–142.
5 TNA, WO 417/60, Casualty Lists – Other Ranks 1120 – 1136, 1943 Apr 28 – 1943 May 17, Expeditionary Forces, (d) North Africa, Wounded, 3rd Bn. Welsh Guards.
6 Philip Brutton, *Ensign in Italy : A Platoon Commander's Story* (Barnsley: Pen & Sword, 1992), p.152.
7 Andrew Gibson-Watt, *An Undistinguished Life* (Chippenham: Antony Rowe Ltd, 1990), p.141.
8 Author.
9 Carole McEntee-Taylor, *A Battle Too Far – The True Story of Rifleman Henry Taylor* (Barnsley: Pen & Sword Military, 2013), p.74.

Chapter 1

10 Topographic map courtesy of Melos Popover.
11 Lieutenant Colonel, A. H. M. Morris, *The Royal Engineers Sixth Armoured Division* (Padova: Tipographia Antoniana, 1946), p.47.
12 Lieutenant Colonel, A. H. M. Morris, *The Royal Engineers Sixth Armoured Division* (Padova: Tipographia Antoniana, 1946), p.43.
13 Alex Bowlby, *The Recollections of Rifleman Bowlby* (London: Cassel Military Paperbacks, 1969, Reprint 2002), p.25.
14 Philip Brutton, *Ensign in Italy : A Platoon Commander's Story* (Barnsley: Pen & Sword, 1992), 152.
15 See also Ken Ford, Ken, *Mailed Fist – 6th Armoured Division at War 1940–45* (Stroud: Sutton Publishing, 2005), p.146.
16 Morris, Lieutenant Colonel, A, H, M, *The Royal Engineers Sixth Armoured Division* (Padova: Tipographia Antoniana, 1946), 30.

Chapter 2

17 TNA, WO 204/10206, War Diary, Reorganisation of Formations – January-December 1944, Memo – Allotment of Formations to Italy, General Alexander, 13 January 1944.
18 TNA, WO 204/10206, War Diary, Reorganisation of Formations – January-December 1944, Memo – Allotment of Formations to Italy, General Alexander, 13 January 1944, pp.1–2.

ENDNOTES

19 TNA, WO 204/10206, War Diary, Reorganisation of Formations – January-December 1944, Memo regarding Reorganisation of Formations in CMF sent to Deputy Chief of Staff AFHQ, 17 January 1944.
20 TNA, WO 204/10206, War Diary, Reorganisation of Formations – January-December 1944, Incoming Message Report from CIGS to General Wilson, 19 January 1944.
21 TNA, WO 204/10206, War Diary, Reorganisation of Formations – January-December 1944, Incoming Message from General Steele to 15 Army Group Generals Gammell and Harding, 10 February 1944.
22 TNA, WO 204/10206, War Diary, Reorganisation of Formations – January-December 1944, Draft Memo to General Steele, DSD War Office from Lieutenant General Gammell, Chief of Staff AFHQ, 17 March 1944.
23 Ken Ford, *Mailed Fist: 6th Armoured Division at War, 1940–45* (Stroud: Sutton Publishing, 2005), p.157.
24 TNA, WO 204/10206, War Diary, Reorganisation of Formations – January-December 1944, Outgoing Message from General Wilson AFHQ, 22 May 1944.
25 TNA, WO 204/10206, War Diary, Reorganisation of Formations – January-December 1944, Outgoing Message For Action, 26 May 1944.
26 TNA, WO 170/610, War Diary 61 Brigade HQ – May-December 1944, Diary Entry 25 May 1944.
27 TNA, WO 204/10206, War Diary, Reorganisation of Formations – January-December 1944, Memo from General Alexander, 8 June 1944.
28 Andrew Gibson-Watt, *An Undistinguished Life* (Chippenham: Antony Rowe Ltd, 1990), p.141.
29 Adam Robson, *Ornito: The Battle For Initiative in The Garigliano Salient, The Second Battalion Coldstream Guards in Italy, February–March 1944* (Self Published, 2018), p.220.
30 TNA, WO 170/1355, War Diary 3rd Battalion Welsh Guards, January-December 1944, Field Return of Officers 29 September 1944.
31 Andrew Gibson-Watt, *An Undistinguished Life* (Chippenham: Antony Rowe Ltd, 1990), pp.142–143.
32 Having been trained together as a Company in North Wales, it was then at No.1 (Guards) Battalion, I.R.T.D at Rotondi, Italy.
33 There are numerous photographs taken of the Scots Guards in Cassino after its fall on 19 May 1944.
34 Michael Curtis, *A Pilgrimage of Remembrance* (Self Published, 2004), p.12.
35 Andrew Gibson-Watt, *An Undistinguished Life* (Chippenham: Antony Rowe Ltd, 1990), pp.144–145.
36 TNA, WO 204/10206, War Diary Reorganisation of formations – January-December 1944, Minutes of AFHQ Meeting 17 January 1944 concerning reorganisation of Forces, page 2, section 7.
37 TNA, WO 170/1355, War Diary 3rd Battalion Welsh Guards, January-December 1944, Diary entries 26–29 May 1944.
38 TNA, WO 170/1355, War Diary 3rd Battalion Welsh Guards, January-December 1944, Diary Entry 30 May 1944.
39 TNA, WO 170/1355, War Diary 3rd Battalion Welsh Guards, January-December 1944, Diary Entry 17 July 1944.
40 Andrew Gibson-Watt, *An Undistinguished Life* (Chippenham: Antony Rowe Ltd, 1990), p.144.
41 Andrew Gibson-Watt, *An Undistinguished Life* (Chippenham: Antony Rowe Ltd, 1990), p.145.
42 Andrew Gibson-Watt, *An Undistinguished Life* (Chippenham: Antony Rowe Ltd, 1990), p.190.
43 Andrew Gibson-Watt, *An Undistinguished Life* (Chippenham: Antony Rowe Ltd, 1990), p,145.
44 TNA, WO 204/10206, War Diary Reorganisation of formations – January-December 1944, Memo to D.I.D War Office from Chief of Staff Lieutenant General J. A. H. Gammell, AFHQ, 17 March 1944.
45 Andrew Gibson-Watt, *An Undistinguished Life* (Chippenham: Antony Rowe Ltd, 1990), p.145.
46 Author's collection, Mathews is currently the subject of ongoing research.
47 Andrew Gibson-Watt, *An Undistinguished Life* (Chippenham: Antony Rowe Ltd, 1990), p/147.
48 The author is unaware of similar changes in the Rifle Battalions of 61st Brigade and thus an order of battle has not been included.
49 Lieutenant Colonel A. H. M. Morris, *The Royal Engineers Sixth Armoured Division* (Padova: Tipographia Antoniana, 1946), p.21.

Chapter 3

50. Alex Bowlby, *The Recollections of Rifleman Bowlby* (London: Cassel Military Paperbacks, 1969, Reprint 2002), p.58.
51. TNA, WO 170/1355, War Diary 3rd Battalion Welsh Guards, January-December 1944. Cassino Relief, Appendix 'A' 2 May 1944.
52. TNA, WO 170/1349, War Diary 3rd Battalion Grenadier Guards, January-December 1944. Battalion Orders part one, Wednesday 3 May 1944.
53. TNA, WO 170/1349, War Diary 3rd Battalion Grenadier Guards, January-December 1944. Battalion Orders, Tuesday 9 May 1944.
54. TNA, WO 170/1355, War Diary 3rd Battalion Welsh Guards, January-December 1944. Operation 'Casino', Appendix B, pp.2 & 3, 4 April 1944.
55. TNA, WO 170/1355, War Diary 3rd Battalion Welsh Guards, January-December 1944. Reliefs at Cassino, Admin for 14–15 April 1944, p.1.
56. Photograph courtesy of Neil Powell, www.battlefieldhistorian.com.
57. TNA, WO 170/1349, War Diary 3rd Battalion Grenadier Guards, January-December 1944. Battalion Orders part one Monday 1 May 1944.
58. Infantry Training, Part VIII. Fieldcraft, Battle Drill, Section and Platoon Tactics 1944, By Command of the Army Council, 4 March 1944. (London: The War Office, 1944), pp.10–11.
59. Close up photographs of weave construction taken by the author's four-and-a-half-year-old son Henry, under instruction.
60. See Imperial War Museum photograph collection references NA1802 and NA1803.
61. Alex Bowlby, *The Recollections of Rifleman Bowlby* (London: Cassel Military Paperbacks, 1969, Reprint 2002), p.52.

Chapter 4

62. I am not aware of any dedicated publication accounting for the development, adoption and manufacture of *Telo Mimetico*.
63. (*Translated from Italian*) Ministry of War S.M. Corps Command, *Instruction on the use of the Waterproofed Camouflage Cloth (Telo Tenda) For Tent Model 1929*, Regulations For Individual Training, 1925 Edition (Rome: State Polygraphic Institute Library, July 1923).
64. Photograph courtesy of Neil Powell, www.battlefieldhistorian.com.
65. Open source image.
66. A demonstration of the use of camouflage at a Sniper School Normandy, 27 July 1944. Photograph courtesy of Neil Powell, www.battlefieldhistorian.com.

Chapter 5

67. TNA, WO 170/1349, War Diary 3rd Battalion Grenadier Guards, January-December 1944, Operation 'Honker' Admin Instructions Appendix A, pp.2–3, 11 May 1944.
68. TNA, WO 170/1355, War Diary 3rd Battalion Welsh Guards, January-December 1944, Warning Order 'Exercise Honker' 'D, 9 May 1944.
69. Adam Robson, *Operations of the 1st Guards Brigade 1942–1945: The Guards at War in Tunisia and Italy* (Self Published, 2019), p.106.
70. TNA, WO 170/1355, War Diary 3rd Battalion Welsh Guards, January-December 1944, Warning Order 'F', 19 May 1944.
71. A photograph of the Welsh Guards moving towards Arce (wearing battledress) is shown in Appendix II.
72. TNA, WO 170/515, War Diary 1st Guards Brigade, January-December 1944. Diary Entry 26 May 1944.
73. Philip Brutton, *Ensign in Italy : A Platoon Commander's Story* (Barnsley: Pen & Sword, 1992), pp.68–69.
74. TNA, WO 170/1355, War Diary 3rd Battalion Welsh Guards, January-December 1944. Diary Entry 29–30 May 1944.
75. Michael Curtis, *A Pilgrimage of Remembrance* (Self Published, 2004), p.36.
76. D. C. Quilter, *No Dishonourable Name: Record of the* 2nd *and* 3rd *Battalions Coldstream Guards in the Second World War* (Manchester: EP Publishing Ltd, 1972), p.87, courtesy of Adam Robson.

77   TNA, WO 170/1348, War Diary 2nd Battalion Coldstream Guards, January-December 1944.
78   The author is grateful to Mr John Herbertson, of Herbertson Fine Arts, for engaging with Carole Cuneo, the daughter of Terence Cuneo, to enable a reproduction of this artwork to be featured within this book.
79   Alex Bowlby, *The Recollections of Rifleman Bowlby* (London: Cassel Military Paperbacks, 1969, Reprint 2002), p.91.
80   TNA, WO 170/1468, War Diary 2nd Battalion Rifle Brigade, May-December 1944. Situation at Nightfall, Daily Account 1 & 2 July 1944, Map Sheet 122 1:50,000.
81   TNA, WO 170/1470, War Diary 10th Battalion Rifle Brigade, May-December 1944. Diary Entry 1 & 2 July 1944.
82   Alex Bowlby, *The Recollections of Rifleman Bowlby* (London: Cassel Military Paperbacks, 1969, Reprint 2002), p.132.
83   TNA, WO 170/610 61, War Diary Brigade HQ, May-December 1944. Diary Entry 26 July 1944.
84   TNA, WO 170/515, War Diary 1st Guards Brigade, January-December 1944, Diary Entry 26 July 1944. Sit-rep as at 2000hrs, 26 July 1944.
85   Michael Curtis, *A Pilgrimage of Remembrance* (Self Published, 2004), p.53.
86   Alex Bowlby, *The Recollections of Rifleman Bowlby* (London: Cassel Military Paperbacks, 1969, Reprint 2002), p.99.
87   TNA, WO 170/515, War Diary 1st Guards Brigade, January-December 1944. C.O.s' Conference 17 July 1944.
88   TNA, War Diary WO 170/610 61, War Diary Brigade HQ, May-December 1944. Diary Entry 16 July 1944.
89   Thank you to Emanuele Moretti.
90   Imperial War Museum, Caption NA16966.
91   TNA, WO 170/515, War Diary 1st Guards Brigade, January-December 1944. Detailed Intentions, night 15–16 July 1944.
92   TNA, War Diary WO 170/1355, War Diary 3rd Battalion Welsh Guards, January-December 1944. Diary Entry 15–16 July 1944.
93   Major L. F. Ellis, *Welsh Guards at War* (London: London Stamp Exchange Ltd, 1989), p.322. It is interesting to note the caption for the image in Philip Brutton,, *Ensign in Italy : A Platoon Commander's Story* (Barnsley: Pen & Sword, 1992), p.85, 'Men of No.1 Company, 3rd Bn. Welsh Guards resting near Arezzo … they are clad in canvas trousers, cap comforters, American khaki shirts and camouflage smocks,' a slight variation.
94   TNA, WO 170/1355, War Diary 3rd Battalion Welsh Guards, January-December 1944. Sit-Rep and Intelligence Summary, 18 July 1944.
95   Ken Ford, *Mailed Fist : 6th Armoured Division at War, 1940–45* (Stroud: Sutton Publishing, 2005), caption within photograph.
96   Brigadier A. C. Gore, D.S.O., *The History of 61 Infantry Brigade May 1944 – June 1945* (Uckfield: The Naval & Military Press Ltd, 1946 Reprint), pp.49–50.
97   Lieutenant Colonel, A. H. M. Morris, *The Royal Engineers, Sixth Armoured Division* (Padova: Tipographia Antoniana, 1946), p.39.
98   Alex Bowlby, *The Recollections of Rifleman Bowlby* (London: Cassel Military Paperbacks, 1969, Reprint 2002), p.168.
99   Alex Bowlby, *The Recollections of Rifleman Bowlby (*London: Cassel Military Paperbacks, 1969, Reprint 2002), p.180.
100 Carole McEntee-Taylor, *A Battle Too Far : The True Story of Rifleman Henry Taylor* (Barnsley: Pen & Sword Military, 2013), p.118.
101 Alex Bowlby, *The Recollections of Rifleman Bowlby* (London: Cassel Military Paperbacks, 1969, Reprint 2002), p.189.
102 Alex Bowlby, *The Recollections of Rifleman Bowlby* (London: Cassel Military Paperbacks, 1969, Reprint 2002), p.211.
103 Andrew Gibson-Watt, *An Undistinguished Life* (Chippenham: Antony Rowe Ltd, 1990), p.159.
104 Andrew Gibson-Watt, *An Undistinguished Life* (Chippenham: Antony Rowe Ltd, 1990), p.154.
105 TNA, WO 170/4982 3rd Battalion Welsh Guards – January-May 1945. Relief Plan 10 February (for 14–15 February 1944).
106 D. C. Quilter, *No Dishonourable Name: Record of the* 2nd *and* 3rd *Battalions Coldstream Guards in the Second World War* (Manchester: EP Publishing Ltd, 1972), p.238. Courtesy of Adam Robson.

Chapter 6

107 *The Second World War 1939–1945, Ordnance Services*, Compiled by the Officers of the Ordnance Directorate (War Office: The War Office, 1950), p.214. Courtesy of Andrew Flindall.

108 Author's collection, Mathews is currently being researched.

109 *The Second World War 1939–1945, Ordnance Services*, Compiled by the Officers of the Ordnance Directorate (War Office: The War Office, 1950), p.215 (upper illustration) and p.216 (lower illustration. Courtesy of Andrew Flindall.

110 TNA, WO170/2866, War Diary Miscellaneous: 'C' Clothing and Repair Factory, February-December 1944. Diary Entry 10 October 1944 (retrospectively covering the period February-September 1944).

111 TNA, WO170/2866, War Diary Miscellaneous: 'C' Clothing and Repair Factory, February-December 1944. Diary Entry 10 October 1944 (retrospectively covering the period February-September 1944).

112 TNA, WO170/2866, War Diary Miscellaneous: 'C' Clothing and Repair Factory, February-December 1944, War Diary Entry 24 October 1944.

113 TNA, WO170/2866, War Diary Miscellaneous: 'C' Clothing and Repair Factory, February-December 1944, Folio 1 Sheet 1, 26 September 1944.

114 TNA, WO170/2866, War Diary Miscellaneous: 'C' Clothing and Repair Factory, February-December 1944. Diary Entry 29 November 1944.

115 TNA, WO170/2866, War Diary Miscellaneous: 'C' Clothing and Repair Factory, February-December 1944. Diary Entries 19–28 October 1944.

116 TNA, WO170/2866, War Diary Miscellaneous: 'C' Clothing and Repair Factory, February-December 1944. Hygiene Report, 26 October 1944

117 TNA, WO170/2866, War Diary Miscellaneous: 'C' Clothing and Repair Factory, February-December 1944, Folio 1 Sheet 4, 26 September 1944.

118 TNA, WO170/2866, War Diary Miscellaneous: 'C' Clothing and Repair Factory, February-December 1944. Education 29 November 1944.

119 TNA, WO170/2866, War Diary Miscellaneous: 'C' Clothing and Repair Factory, February-December 1944, 'C' Clothing & Repair Factory, Folio 1 Sheet 3, 26 September 1944.

120 TNA, WO170/2866, War Diary Miscellaneous: 'C' Clothing and Repair Factory, February-December 1944, 'C' Clothing & Repair Factory, Folio 1 Sheet 5, 26 September 1944.

121 TNA, WO170/2866, War Diary Miscellaneous: 'C' Clothing and Repair Factory, February-December 1944. Field Return of Other Ranks, 30 September 1944.

Chapter 8

122 Alex Bowlby, *The Recollections of Rifleman Bowlby* (London: Cassel Military Paperbacks, 1969, Reprint 2002), p.61.

123 Michael Curtis, *A Pilgrimage of Remembrance* (Self Published, 2004), p.53.

124 Alex Bowlby, *The Recollections of Rifleman Bowlby* (London: Cassel Military Paperbacks, 1969, Reprint 2002), p.132.

125 *Small Arms Training, Volume 1, Pamphlet No. 4, Light Machine Gun* (London: H.M. Stationery Office, 1937), p.15

Appendices

126 Ken Ford, *Mailed Fist: 6th Armoured Division at War 1940–45* (Stroud: Sutton Publishing, 2005), caption within photograph plates.

127 Lieutenant Colonel, A. H. M. Morris, *The Royal Engineers Sixth Armoured Division* (Padova: Tipographia Antoniana, 1946), p.97.

128 TNA, WO 170/1349, War Diary 3rd Battalion Grenadier Guards, January-December 1944, Battalion Orders Part One, Monday 22 May 1944

129 Morris, Lieutenant Colonel, A, H, M, *The Royal Engineers Sixth Armoured Division* (Padova: Tipographia Antoniana, 1946), 75.

130 (Translated from Italian) Ministry of War S. M. Corps Command, *Instruction on the use of the Waterproofed Camouflage Cloth (Telo Tenda) For Tent Model 1929*, Regulations For Individual Training, 1925 Edition (Rome: State Polygraphic Institute Library, Rome, July 1929), pp.156–159.

Bibliography

Books, Published

Bowlby, Alex, *The Recollections of Rifleman Bowlby*, (London, Cassel Military Paperbacks, 1969, Reprint 2002)

Borasarello, J. & Lassus, D., *Camouflaged Uniforms of the Wehrmacht*, (London, ISO Publications, 1998)

Bouchery, Jean, *From D-Day to VE-Day, The British Soldier, Volume 1 – Uniforms, Insignia, Equipments* (*sic*), (Paris: Histoire & Collections, 2006)

Bouchery, Jean, *From D-Day to VE-Day, The British Soldier, Volume 2 – Organisation, Armament, Tanks & Vehicles*, (Paris: Histoire & Collections, 2003)

Brayley, Martin J., & Ingram, Richard, *Khaki Drill & Jungle Green, British Tropical Uniforms 1939–45. In Colour Photographs*, (Marlborough: The Crowood Press Ltd, 2000)

Brayley Martin J., *The British Army 1939–45 (2) Middle East & Mediterranean, Men-at-Arms 368*, (Oxford: Osprey Publishing, 2002)

Brayley, Martin J. & Ingram, Richard, *The World War II Tommy – British Army Uniforms European Theatre1939–45. In Colour Photographs*, (Marlborough: The Crowood Press Ltd, 1998)

Brutton, Philip, *Ensign In Italy : A Platoon Commander's Story*, (Barnsley: Pen & Sword, 1992)

Chappell, Mike, *The Guards Divisions 1914–45, Elite Series 61*, (London: Osprey Publishing, 1995)

Curtis, Michael, *A Pilgrimage of Remembrance*, (Self Published, 2004)

Dethick, Janet Kinrade, *The Trasimene Line, June – July 1944*, Revised Edition, (Cittadi Castello: Fondazione Ranieri di Sorbello, 2013)

Ellis, Major L. F., *Welsh Guards at War*, (London: London Stamp Exchange Ltd, 1989)

Ford, Ken, *Mailed Fist : 6th Armoured Division at War 1940–45*, (Stroud: Sutton Publishing, 2005)

Forty, George, *Battle for Monte Cassino*, (Hersham: Ian Allen Publishing Ltd, 2004)

Gibson-Watt, Andrew, *An Undistinguished Life*, (Chippenham: Antony Rowe Ltd, 1990)

Gore, Brigadier A. C., D.S.O., *The History of 61 Infantry Brigade May 1944 – June 1945*, (Uckfield: The Naval & Military Press Ltd (reprint), 1946)

Holland, James, *Italy's Sorrow : A Year of War 1944–45*, (London: Harper Press, 2008)

Mansolas, Angelos N., *The Reaper's Harvesting Summer – 12th SS Panzer Division 'Hitlerjugend' In Normandy*, (Sroud: Fonthill Media Limited, 2021)

McEntee-Taylor, Carole, *A Battle Too Far : The True Story of Rifleman Henry Taylor*, (Barnsley: Pen & Sword Military, 2013)

McKenzie, William I., *Diary of a D-Day Dodger*, (Clackmannan, Clackmannan District Libraries, 1989)

Morris, Lieutenant Colonel A. H. M., *The Royal Engineers – Sixth Armoured Division, (*Padova, Tipographia Antoniana, 1946)

Peterson, Daniel, *Wehrmacht Camouflage Uniforms & Post-War Derivatives*, (Marlborough, The Crowood Press Ltd, 2004)

Quilter, D. C., *No Dishonourable Name: Record of the 2nd and* 3rd *Battalions Coldstream Guards in the Second World War*, (Manchester, EP Publishing Ltd, 1972)

Retallack, John, *The Welsh Guards*, (London, Frederick Warne (Publishers) Ltd, 1981)

Robson, Adam, *Operations of the 1st Guards Brigade 1942–1945: The Guards at War in Tunisia and Italy*, (Self Published, 2019)

Robson, Adam, *Ornito : The Battle for Initiative in The Gargliano Salient, The Second Battalion Coldstream Guards in Italy February–March 1944*, (Self Published, 2018)
Ryder, Rowland, *Oliver Leese*, (London: Hamish Hamilton Ltd, 1987)
Steven, Andrew & Amodio, Peter, *Waffen-SS Uniforms in Colour Photographs*, (Marlborough, The Crowood Press Ltd, 2003)
The Second World War 1939–1945, Ordnance Services, Compiled by the Officers of the Ordnance Directorate, (London: The War Office, 1950)

Booklets and Pamphlets, Published

Infantry Training, Part VIII. Fieldcraft, Battle Drill, Section and Platoon Tactics 1944, By Command of the Army Council, (London: The War Office, 4 March 1944. 26/G.S. Publications 10/76)
Notes from Theatres of War, No. 20: Italy 1943/44, Prepared under the direction of The Chief of the Imperial General Staff, (London: The War Office, May, 1945. 26/GS Publications 14/13)
Ministry of War S. M. Corps Command, *Instruction on the use of the Waterproofed Camouflage Cloth (Telo Tenda) For Tent Model 1929*, Regulations For Individual Training, 1925 Edition, (Rome: State Polygraphic Institute Library, July 1923, *Translation*)
Small Arms Training, Volume 1, Pamphlet No. 4, Light Machine Gun, (London: His Majesty's Stationery Office, 1937)

Manuscripts, The National Archives

WO 170, War Office: Central Mediterranean Forces, (British Element):
WO 170/515 1st Guards Brigade, January-December 1944
WO 170/610 61st Brigade HQ, May-December 1944
WO 170/1348 2nd Battalion Coldstream Guards, January-December 1944
WO 170/1349 3rd Battalion Grenadier Guards, January-December 1944
WO 170/1355 3rd Battalion Welsh Guards, January-December 1944
WO 170/1468 2nd Battalion Rifle Brigade, May-July 1944
WO 170/1469 7th Battalion Rifle Brigade, May-July 1944
WO 170/1470 10th Battalion Rifle Brigade, May-July 1944
WO 170/2866 Miscellaneous: 'C' Clothing and Repair Factory, February-December 1944
WO 170/4982 3rd Battalion Welsh Guards, January-May 1945
WO 204, War Office: Allied Forces, Mediterranean Theatre:
Military Headquarters Papers, Second World War, G3 – Organisation Subsection. Reorganisation of formations: WO 204/10206 Reorganisation of Formations – January-December 1944
WO 417, War Office, Casualty Lists:
WO 417/60 – Other Ranks 1120 – 1136, 1943 Apr 28 – 1943 May 17

About The Author

Gareth Scanlon is a Police Contact Management Strategic Leader. He is a fluent Welsh speaker as a native of the Amman Valley in South West Wales where he lives today with his wife and 5-year-old son. He is an avid Second World War historian and is a published nature photographer.